UP THE SHORE

38 Aerial view of Cognashene area showing the Freddy Channel

A timeless story of Georgian Bay

By
Juanita Rourke

Sincerely
Juanita Rourke

Up The Shore Enterprises

and

MIDLAND PRINTERS
1995
MIDLAND, ONTARIO
CANADA

UP THE SHORE

Published by: Up The Shore Enterprises

ISBN: 0 - 9 6 9 8 9 4 7 - 0 8

Cover photograph, Georgian Bay by: Bev Keefe

Edited by: Bonnie Rourke

Printed and bound in Canada

I would like to thank :
The Ontario Arts Council for their assistance.
The Midland Free Press for permission to use some material
I published in their paper.
W.A. Cranston for his encouragement for so many years.
Ritchie With, editor, writer, friend who urged me to write this book long ago.

For their personal contributions to this endeavor I thank:
Mary Paradis, Peter Grisdale, Emery O'Rourke, Jim Wallace, Jack Lamoureux, Bev Keefe, Joe Patenaude, Gary Rourke and Frank Powell, Q.C.
and, for their support throughout, all my children.

DEDICATION

To the People of the Shore

62

Juanita Rourke

Juanita Rourke

Juanita Rourke was born in Victoria Harbour, Ontario. Her mother, Euphemia Tait was a Scottish war bride, her father Charles Myers, a Canadian woodsman who's grandfather was a United Empire Loyalist. Juanita had an older brother Allie, born in Scotland. Like their father, they grew up in the wilderness that their grandfather William had pioneered. Juanita's writing talent appeared early, writing poems and childrens plays by the age of seven. She attended a one room school in Moon River and finished her education by correspondence courses. But it was after her marriage to Frank Rourke and the birth of her children that her writing career began in earnest. Writing for the Midland Free Press she progressed from writing a social type of column to chronicalling the daily and weekly events of the people of the shore and her life on Minnicog Island, "...the Island that had intrigued me every time I passed by it." Few of us are so fortunate to both realize and enjoy our dreams.

This book summarizes both her writing career and her life up the shore on Georgian Bay.

Table of Contents

The Stories

The Stories, continued

Chapter

Page

The Pictures

Picture Number and Title   **Page**
In order of appearance

The Pictures, continued

The Pictures, continued

Picture Number and Title   **Page**
In order of appearance

ç

1

The Move to Minnicog

1 The Great Manor House of Colonel Cautley
The Minnicog Hotel during its resort days
The Administration Building for the Navy League of Canada

It was early fall, 1943. The sun was slanting westward. Haze of late September hung over the eastern shoreline of Georgian Bay. We were nearing the end of our trip down the shore from Moon River. Ahead lay the island of Minnicognashene[1] where we would live for the next fifteen years. The houseboat swayed slightly over the long lazy swells between Kindersley Island and the north end of Minnicog. I walked to the front of the houseboat to check the tow line. Even though Frank, in the boat ahead, kept a constant watch on it, the line had broken once during our journey down "the shore"[2]. We were wary of it happening again.

I walked to the back door to check on the small wooden inboard we were towing behind. It had the habit of running its bow under the overhang of the houseboat when it rode a big swell.

The baby stirred in the carriage which kept running back and forth across the living room when I forgot to put the brake on. Our other three children were weary of the confinement. The horse, tied in the bedroom, stomped his feet restlessly.

I was excited about the idea of living on an island that intrigued me every time I had passed by it. At last I could explore the building with towering white chimneys. A landmark on the shore for many years.

Frank swung in between a reef of shoals and John's Island. He hurried to the stern of the boat to haul in the heavy tow line. Back at the wheel he eased us gently

---

1. Minnicognashene is also called Minnicog.
2. "The shore" is a term used to describe the area anywhere among the Georgian Bay islands between Midland and Parry Sound. "Up The Shore" is where we all went, some of us to live, some of us to holiday and it will *always* be in the hearts of any of us who have gone "Up The Shore".

alongside the main dock. Glen, our five year old, was out on the dock as quickly as his dad. He helped to hold the line until Frank got the boat and both ends of the houseboat tied up. I stood on the long dock holding Gail and Gary by the hand. I looked up towards the smooth granite rocks and the pine trees that are forever twisted eastward on Georgian Bay and knew I was home.

The first thing to do before we could go exploring was to bring the horse ashore. Frank untied him and led him through the living room out onto the deck. The scow was almost level with the dock so it was an easy step up onto the dock. Frank led him off with the horse's hooves making a hollow sound on the wooden decking. Frank let him go as soon as they reached the end of the dock. The horse was as glad to be free as I was to get him out of the house.

Frank checked the lines on the boat and the houseboat, making sure they were secure. He gathered Bonnie, our four month old, out of her carriage and we went ashore to go up on the island to see our new home. The first thing I noticed about the Winter House was the north wall was built of cement and stone, the rest of it was clapboard with a wide verandah sweeping across the front. When Frank opened the door, we had to caution the children about glass strewn on the floor. The house had not been a home for some time but it appealed to me immediately with its French doors looking eastward towards Beausoleil Island. The view was magnificent, islands clustered in the blue waters, the sumacs flaming crimson against the grey granite rocks. When we meandered back to the houseboat to make supper I knew it would not take long to make the house into a home. I was anxious to get started.

It was difficult to realize. I was about to do the thing I had been dreaming about ever since I was a youngster in Moon River. I would be living on the fringe of the islands where the waters of the Bay stretched out to meet the horizon. Not everyone would be as thrilled as I was to live on an island twelve miles from the nearest town with long stretches of water between myself and neighbours. I was raised on the eastern shore of Georgian Bay and after Frank and I were married I tried living in town with houses and people all around me, where I could go to a movie show any day of the week or window shop along the main street of the town. I did all that and found my feet always took me to the dock where I stood and gazed longingly at the Bay. Whenever the opportunity came we would take to the boat and head up the shore. That is where we belonged.

The opportunity to live on the island came in a roundabout way. When Frank came back from overseas and was discharged from the army he took the job of running the supply boat carrying supplies to the Navy League Sea Cadet Camps on Minnicognashene and Beausoleil Islands. It was a natural thing for him to do since he had run a floating grocery store amongst the islands for a number of years before the war broke out. The supply boat took groceries to the docks of the tourist population during the summer months. It saved them the bother of leaving their summer homes to run into town for food supplies.

Supplying the Sea Cadet Camps was different. There was a contract for food supplies given to a store and these supplies were delivered to the Camps every day with the exception of Sunday. It was in August when the architect for the Camps caught a ride with Frank to Minnicog. He happened to mention the Navy League was looking for a man to look after the Camps. During the course of the conversation he asked Frank if he would be interested. Frank told him he certainly would be but had to fulfill his contract with the supply boat company which meant he would not be available until Labour Day. He applied for the job, was interviewed and was told at that time he had the job.

The chance to go to Minnicog was just what we had been looking for. Living in town was alien to both of us and this was our way back to the freedom of the shore.

When Frank laid the supply boat up in September there was no definite word from Navy headquarters about the job at Minnicog. Frank wasn't a person to sit around waiting. He bought a houseboat from contractors who were doing the building and repairs at the Sea Cadet Camps. The house was on a sixty-foot scow and was used for cooking and sleeping accommodation for the workmen.

In the meantime the painter who did all the exterior and interior painting at the Camps asked Frank if he would work for him after the supply boat was laid up. Frank agreed since it would be a good way to earn some money until he had definite word about the job as caretaker and maintenance supervisor at the Camps.

We had moved out of our house in town on a Friday afternoon. Setting up housekeeping in the houseboat was quite an experience. There were bunk beds built in one of the bedrooms which accommodated the children, our bed was set up in the other. The living area was large and there were rough cupboards in the kitchen. We spent the night moored at the dock in Midland. My parents found it most unusual. It was my Scottish born mother's first time sleeping on the water. They had come down the Bay from Moon River to spend a few days with us not knowing we were about to move. When morning came they were more than ready to get into their boat and head for the sanctuary of the shore.

Frank had our boat running when they left. He secured the tow rope, checked the little boat behind the scow and untied the houseboat from the dock. We were underway before eight o'clock, our destination, some bay near Beausoleil Island. The children thought the whole thing was exciting as they walked around in the house watching the water surrounding us. They were learning at an early age they were born to parents who did strange things, usually on the spur of the moment.

The wind was westerly, the sun bright in the eastern sky. The houseboat rocked gently in the gap in front of Brébeuf lighthouse. I bathed the baby as we maneuvered our way through the Bulls Eye and Gendron's Channel. Frank was in the boat alone and he had forgotten his tobacco in the houseboat. When we came abreast of Minnicog Island he idled the motor, walked to the stern of the boat and pulled on the tow line until he was alongside the houseboat.

"I forgot my tobacco," he hollered.

I found it on the table and took it out to him. He sat on the edge of the boat stuffing his pipe with tobacco. While I had been doing the household chores he had been thinking. I knew there was something on his mind. He struck a match and puffed on his pipe for a few minutes. He took the pipe from his mouth, held it in his hand and looked towards Minnicog.

"You know," he said, "I have nothing definite about the job. We can't live out here in a houseboat for the winter. I think I should take you on up to Moon River and come back down myself to paint for Lalonde."

I looked at the island I had expected to live on. I looked at Frank and I agreed. When Frank made up his mind I knew I could trust his decision.

We ran into a little problem between Eaton's Island and Split Rock. There was quite a sea rolling and Frank had to check the boat down because the tow line started to sever. I kept watching the rope pull apart until there were only two strands left. He knew it was going to break so he pulled into a dock at Split Rock and tied up. We would stay until the wind dropped. It could have been a few hours or a week, but we did not worry because we had plenty of supplies aboard.

We ate lunch with the sound of waves lapping against the side of the scow. Frank filled a kettle with water from the Bay and we heated it on the little oil stove. After the dishes were washed we took the children for a walk over the rough rocks. There was the smell of pine trees and juniper in the air. Afterwards Frank went off in the boat to check the cottage of a good friend of his from Toronto. When he came back he held up a heavy new tow line.

"Just what we need," he said with a grin, "the Doctor told me to use whatever I needed. I will return it when I come back down."

He tied it to the scow and to the stern of the boat. He looked out at the Bay. "Come on," he said, "the wind is dropping."

The scow rode the swells gently around Moose Deer Point. The children settled in their beds. I sat in the rocking chair feeding the baby, watching the dark shoreline slip silently by. We had no further trouble with tow lines. At midnight we came alongside Father Myers dock in Woods Bay. We tied up the boat lying on the outside of the scow and fell into bed exhausted.

It was a very surprised Father Myers who looked out of the kitchen window the next morning at six o'clock. "Come and see what is at the dock!" he called to my mother.

The children were up and about early. They were bubbling with excitement over the fact they were at Nanna's and Gramps island. When they were dressed, they scampered off the dock and up to the house. My parents were delighted to have them. The day was spent moving the houseboat around the point into a snug little bay. Frank put down a gangplank so we could reach the shore easily.

It was a fine September week and we enjoyed a holiday. Frank spent some time making things more comfortable for us before leaving to go down to Minnicog to paint. We took a boat trip up river to visit the Moon River Falls to watch the trickle of water running where once a mighty waterfall lunged over the rocky cliffs. We were invited to a dance at Sans Souci on the Friday night, a gathering of the shore people about to celebrate the end of a busy season with the tourists. It meant old time square dancing to the tune of a fiddler, a hearty lunch at midnight and a chance to spend an evening with old friends. There was no concern about getting a baby sitter for the children, everyone took their children along and bedded them down at the house where the dance was being held.

Meanwhile, Mr. Lindsay, the man who had interviewed Frank for the job at Minnicog, started looking for him on the Monday. The job was confirmed and Mr. Lindsay was anxious for Frank to take over the position. He arrived in Midland the day after we left for Moon River and couldn't find us. We had told no one we were leaving. Finally, on Thursday, Louis Dusome, who had been looking after the Camps and a man who knew the shore very well, said: "I bet he went up to his father-in-law's place in Moon River."

It was four o'clock on Friday afternoon when we heard the hum of a boat coming through the Captain Allen Straits. Frank stood on the rocks in front of my parents house watching the white hulled boat with its glassed in varnished top coming towards the dock.

"That's the boat *Minnicog* from the Cadet Camps," he exclaimed as it approached.

Louis Dusome in his seaman's uniform was at the wheel. When he pulled alongside the dock Mr. Lindsay stepped out. Frank was there to meet him.

"Why didn't you leave word where you were going?" Mr Lindsay asked when he shook Frank's hand. "We have been looking for you all week."

There was a feeling of excitement amongst all of us. The visitors were ushered up the path to Mother Myers house where she bustled around preparing supper. Plans to attend the dance at Sans Souci were cancelled.

4 The *Minnicog*

"We want you to take over the Camps as soon as possible," Mr. Lindsay told Frank.

"I will be there on Monday morning," Frank assured him.

The children and I went back to our houseboat while Frank spent the evening at my parents house discussing the many details of his new job. There was much involved. Minnicog was the largest Sea Cadet Camp in Canada. It had been christened the Princess Alice Camp earlier that year by the Governor General's wife, Princess Alice, the Duchess of Athlone. Frank's job also included caring for the Sea Cadet Camp on Beausoleil Island, known as the Queen Elizabeth Camp, named after Queen Elizabeth, the wife of King George the sixth, the reigning monarch at the time.

Each Camp had many buildings to look after and maintain. There were generating plants for electricity since there was no hydro on the islands of the eastern shore of Georgian Bay until much later. Pump houses with gasoline operated pumps for the water supply and miles of pipes had to be connected in the spring and disconnected in the fall. Frank had a busy future caring for and maintaining these establishments. When he finally came home at eleven o'clock we had many things to talk about.

The official from the Navy League and his party spent the night at Mother and Father Myers house. Frank joined them for breakfast and walked them to the dock when they were ready to leave. The children and I watched them leave and listened to the hum of the motor, a hum I was to listen for so many times in the years to come. We gathered in the house to talk excitedly about our future. Frank and my father talked business. We needed a horse to use on the island. There were two big ice houses to fill with ice during the winter months. Horses were used to pull the loaded sleds and were also the only means of transportation in the winter months.

My Dad had a horse to sell. It belonged to my brother Allie who was serving overseas with the Air Force. It was young with slender legs and a sleek brown coat. His name was Billy and he was more of a pet than anything else. Frank bought the horse and that is why I traveled down Georgian Bay with a horse in the house.

42 Charlie and Phemie Myers

Frank decided to leave us in Moon River for a week while he went down and took over the Camps from Louis Dusome. He left on Monday morning to meet Mr. Dusome at the Camp. He wasn't there so Frank went on into Midland. As he was pulling into Midland, Mr. Dusome was just coming down to the dock to get into his boat. He and Frank returned to Minnicog together where the Camps were turned over to Frank.

After the necessary papers were signed Frank ran him back into Midland. When Frank returned to the island, they were his to look after, a job that lasted for over a decade until the Camps were closed down. He spent the rest of the week in his new kingdom, then came for us on the Friday to take us down to our home at Minnicognashene.

We left Moon river the next morning just at daylight. The horse had been coaxed aboard, much against its will, and tied in our bedroom. Dad supplied us with enough hay and oats to keep the horse happy until we reached our destination. He helped Frank turn the houseboat around and tie the tow line to the tow boat. The wind was in the south-south east and it started to blow a little harder as we made our way out the channel. When we reached the Hole in the Wall near Manitou the wind had picked up so we pulled into Starvation Bay and tied up for the day.

Frank left us there to go up to see his friend Captain Fred Wallace[3.] who had a summer hotel known as Manitou Inn. Frank had gone to buy some milk for the children and some eggs. While he was there Captain Wallace offered to give him a hand to tow the house boat down to Cross Rock which is

---

3. Fred Wallace was Captain of the Midland City for several years . He later operated the Manitou Inn for several more years.

down back of Split Rock. He figured we would make faster time around the rough Moose Deer Point with two boats towing the houseboat.

We didn't enjoy our night aboard. Frank and I slept on the couch in the living room because the horse occupied the bedroom. Frank cleaned up the floor often with the shovel but that didn't get rid of the strong odor. Billy was restless through the night. He pawed the floor with his front feet and stomped with his hind feet. Baby Bonnie was equally restless in her carriage. When daylight came I was glad to be up with the children preparing breakfast while Frank checked the lines on the scow and the small boat we were towing behind.

We pulled out of Starvation Bay at eight o'clock. Frank had his tow line on the scow and Fred had his tow line on Frank's boat. It was a cool morning with choppy waves. Steam rolled from the exhausts of the boats. I stood by the window watching while the boats pulled the lines taut. We moved slowly up the narrow channel, past Manitou Inn and through the buoys at Jubilee. The houseboat started to rock on the swells sweeping in off Georgian Bay. I put Gary and Gail on the couch because they kept falling when they tried to stand. I made sure the brake was on the baby carriage and went to the back door to look at the little boat we were towing behind.

There was a moment of excitement when the nose of the boat ran under the overhang of the scow. Glen, the five year old, clasped his hands in anxiety. "Now we are in a hell'ov'a, I mean heck of a mess!" He exclaimed. The language problem was one of the reasons I was happy to leave town.

3 My brother Allie and Billy

There was more excitement to come. When we were off Moose Point the tow line from the houseboat to Frank's boat broke. That meant the children and I were drifting helplessly off the rocky, shoal infested shore. Frank reacted quickly. He threw the engine into neutral, climbed over the windshield of his boat and unfastened the line between the two boats. The boat was pitching and spray was coming over the bow. He scrambled back to the wheel in a matter of seconds, circled back and picked up the line. I was busy keeping a wary eye on him and another on the shoreline. In a matter of minutes he had the line straightened up and tied securely to the stern of the boat. Captain Wallace was standing by.

41 Captain Fred Wallace

(picture courtesy Jim Wallace)

He had pulled his tow line in and was standing in the back of his boat when Frank was ready. He tied his line to the bow of our boat and, with less power, they towed a little easier with no further trouble with the lines breaking. The wind seemed to drop a little the further we came down the channel. Fred Wallace left us at Cross Rock. He untied the line from Frank's boat, waved and headed back to Manitou.

Frank kept towing steadily. We did not stop for lunch, he dropped back alongside the scow and I handed him some sandwiches. He was ever on the alert, watching the weather, the passage ahead and the tow line behind. It was mid-afternoon when we were abreast of Go Home Bay. The swells were big and we were pitching a lot. The horse in the bedroom was stomping and snorting again and the children were more restless than ever. We ran very slowly, heading for Cognashene. When we gained the shelter of the islands Frank gave the boat almost full throttle. Above the trees we could see the tall white chimneys of the main house at Minnicog.

At four o'clock we pulled alongside the dock at the Princess Alice Sea Cadet Camp. When I stepped out on the dock of the "Place where the blueberries grow," I knew a dream had come true.

47 Cross Rock

(picture by Bev Keefe)

2

A Horse In The House

Did you ever go sailing
With a horse in the house
Stomping and snorting
And jumping about?

It happened to me
One September day
When I sailed down the shore
Of Georgian Bay

The houseboat we sailed in
My children and me
Rolled and swayed on the swells
When we passed One Tree

The horse in the house
Didn't like that one bit
He pulled on his bridle
And started to kick

"Whoa! Whoa!"
I hollered, seized with fright
If that horse broke loose
We were in a sad plight

Stormbound I slept
With that horse in the house
He in the bedroom
And I on the couch

When dawn streaked the sky
We were on our way
I couldn't eat breakfast
But he munched on his hay

We didn't stop once
'Til we reached Minnicog Bay
That horse left my house
With a leap and a neigh

A horse in the house
Is something to see
But never again
Did he go sailing with me!

J.R.

3

Minnicognashene

Pine clad, irregular in shape, Minnicognashene Island is one of the famous Thirty Thousand Islands of Georgian Bay, lying west, nor'west of Beausoleil Island National Park. It was remote enough from the mainland to appeal to me. There were twelve miles of water between it and the town of Midland, a town known far and wide as the home of the famous Martyr's Shrine standing high on the hill overlooking the Wye River and the Bay.

Minnicog is a wind and water eroded foot of one of the oldest mountains in the world. Many thousands of years ago it was covered by a succession of glaciers. They squeezed and scoured the mountain through the ages. When the glaciers drew back for the final time, water from the melting ice formed a huge lake known to the Indians as Attigouautan. The water filled in around the eroded mountains forming many islands, including Minnicognashene.

The Huron Indians called the island: "The place where blueberries grow." Their birch bark canoes touched its shores. From time to time these farmers and fishermen, these hunters who occupied North Simcoe, camped on Minnicog. They knew its beauty and the magnificent sunsets viewed from the summit.

There is no doubt the great explorer Samuel de Champlain passed by Minnicog when he came with his Huron friends across the shimmering bay he called "La Mer Douce" - The Freshwater Sea. His Indian friends were anxious to show him their great domain lying between

Georgian Bay and Lake Couchiching where they dwelt in
large log longhouses and cultivated the land. Pumpkins,
corn and many other vegetables grew in this "promised
land."

Champlain led the first white colonization of the land, a
colonization that came to a fiery end in less than a decade
when the Iroquois laid siege to Fort Saint Marie. The flames
could have been seen from Minnicog and the smell of smoke
would have hung over the restless waters surrounding it.
The Hurons dream of peace and the French dream of an
empire faded forever as the last remnants of a proud nation
and the few remaining French fled the scene of plunder and
devastation.

For the next one hundred and fifty years Minnicog and
Georgian Bay were quiet. The gulls circled its shores and the
black ducks nested undisturbed in the marshes. The
blueberries shriveled on the bushes and the pine trees grew
tall. The only sounds were those of nature: a "nor'wester"
piling breakers against the shore, wind sighing through the
twisted pines, the howl of a winter blizzard enveloping the
island chain. Perhaps the Objibwa came to its shores in their
birch bark canoes.

It was a war of a different nature that brought the white
man back to Georgian Bay. They battled with warships and
guns this time, not with tomahawks. Instead of the blood
curdling cry of the Iroquois it was the sound of gunpowder
disturbing the tranquility of the Bay.

The Naval and Military Establishment at
Penetanguishene[4] was only nine miles away across the

---

4.   Penetanguishene is known as Penetang.

water. The island of Minnicog sheltered warships at one time
or another. A cannon ball lifted from the bay at Minnicog
was a relic of those turbulent days when the United States
invaded Canada. Men and supplies were sent out past
Minnicog to the garrison at Drummond Island, men in ships
who defeated the Americans and helped make Canada what
it is today.

The 1800's found the silence gone forever from the shores
surrounding Minnicognashene. White settlers moved into
the land of the Huron. Men in little, hand made sailing
sloops began to ply the lakes. One of those would have been
my grandfather, William Myers, from southern Ontario,
searching out his sanctuary on the shore where the trees
grew tall, the red deer were plentiful and where there was a
harvest of furs in the lakes of the back country. It was a virgin
land and he was one of the first to realize its potential.

After the shipyards were established swift, beautiful ships
appeared on Georgian Bay. Their white sails billowed in the
wind as they plied the channels around Minnicog carrying
lumber and supplies. Pure stands of white pine grew in
abundance on the islands and the straggling shoreline of the
Bay. By 1872 lumbermen had cleared the timber off
Minnicog. For a while there was the sound of the axe biting
into the pine, the hum of saws and the falling timber, tall and
straight, crashing down. There were voices of the teamsters
talking to the horses as they skidded the logs to the shore.
When spring came the logs were rolled into Georgian Bay,
surrounded by booms, huge timbers linked together by
chains, to be towed away to the sawmills where they were
sawed into the finest lumber.

Minnicog was sixty feet high at the summit, but trees added greatly to its height. Its shoreline was indented with several coves and bays. An island worth possessing, a good place for a summer residence, something which was starting to occur amongst the Thirty Thousand Islands. The two hundred and thirty acres of some of the hardest granite in the world was viewed by many passing by in tugs to the mill town of Muskoka Mills near the mouth of the Musquash River.

One such person was Walter John Keating, a Penetanguishene lawyer. The island was Indian land granted to Mr. Keating. Date of Patent was 19 September 1885.

The neighbouring Governor Island was granted Patent of Letters to Hon. John Beverley Robinson at the same time. According to local history, a Sir Roderick Cameron of New York bought Minnicognashene for three hundred dollars in 1897 from Walter Keating. He later sold it to William Griscom of Philadelphia for three hundred and fifty dollars.

William Griscom built at least part of the great Manor. It was built on the very summit of the island, three stories high, with balconies, wide sweeping verandahs and twin white chimneys which became a familiar landmark on the shore. A widow's walk[5] on the top of the building commanded a view of the surrounding waters as far as the eye could see. An Irishman, Colonel Cautley, who had served with the British Imperial Army, a veteran of the war in India, found his way to Georgian Bay and in 1901 bought the "Place where the blueberries grow" from the widow of the late

5. This widow's walk was gone by the time we lived on Minnicog.

William Griscom for five thousand dollars. It was he who built the complex that became one of the show places amongst the Thirty Thousand Islands.

A road was built through the swamps and along the rocky ridges to the north dock three quarters of a mile from the main house. To this day you can see the impression made in the rocks by the old iron rimmed wagon wheels. Logs of the corduroy road can be found in the swamps. Along this road the Colonel and his sisters would ride in their horse drawn carriage to meet their guests who would arrive by steamer from Penetanguishene, steamers such as the *John Lee*, the *Waubic* and, later, the *City of Toronto*. Having dropped their passengers, these boats would continue on their daily trips along the Inside Channel to Parry Sound.

The Colonel had many invited guests. They came from Toronto on the Grand Trunk train which left Union Station at eight o'clock in the morning. Lunch was eaten at the station in Allandale where they changed trains and arrived at Penetanguishene at one thirty in the afternoon. The train station was at the dock and from there the guests boarded the passenger boat for the trip to Minnicog.

The interior of the Manor was finished in dark wood. There were six, nine foot French doors in the living room. The ceiling soared to a height of fifteen feet. A wide stairway swept up to the second floor. Marble topped washstands and built-in tin bathtubs with matched lumber provided great comfort in the bathrooms. Many doors opened off the long carpeted corridor into bedrooms furnished with brass beds, mirrored dressers and wardrobes. China commode sets with

5 The *Midland City*

6 The *City of Dover*

floral designs sat on every washstand. A fireplace in several of the bedrooms provided warmth on a cool evening.

The downstairs furnishings were exquisite. Velvet curtains hung at the French doors. A hand carved side table from Arabia, inlaid with ivory, an oval rosewood table and carved love seats were part of the decor. Silver, pewter and beautiful crystal were used in the dining room which was furnished with massive hand carved oak furniture. The dining room table stretched out to accommodate twenty-four guests. Fires danced in the brick fireplaces.

It seems destiny ruled that Minnicognashene was to play host to many people. The place became so popular that Colonel Cautley decided to take in paying guests. He built more and larger buildings to accommodate those who wanted to spend the summer months on his island. He built the Upper Annex, a two storey building with many bedrooms opening off long central corridors. Verandahs stretched the full length of the front of the building. Minnicog was to become the most luxurious summer resort on Georgian Bay.

He built the Winter House on the side hill, the one that would become our home. The north wall was built of cement and stone against the cold northwesterly winds that prevail on Georgian Bay in the winter. There was a red brick fireplace in the living room and stove pipe holes through the ceiling for the wood burning box stove made of cast iron and the wood burning cook stove in the kitchen. It was in this building, with its five bedrooms, living and dining rooms and kitchen, that Colonel Cautley sometimes spent part of the winter months.

7 Upper Annex

8 Octagonal Building or Dance Hall

The Colonel was killed by a streetcar in Buffalo, New York during the winter of 1908. The date of his death is chiseled in a rock close to the main building. A niece and a nephew inherited the island. The Toronto General Trust Company, as executor of the estate, operated it as a summer resort for them.

The following years saw great expansion. Captain Malcomson, part owner of the Welland House in Saint Catherines, was made manager of the resort. A lower Annex was built near the Winter House. The Green Cottage, with six bedrooms and a living room with a fireplace, overlooked the bay towards the east. Cage Cottage, similar in size, was built looking south towards Midland Point. The Big Ark and the Little Ark were nestled close to the water and the Rock Cottage was built astride a rocky point with a dock built out to it.

Whole families would move into these cottages for the full summer season. Sir William Mullock, the venerable gentleman with the long beard who was Canada's Post Master General, raised his family at Minnicog during the summer months. The Stauntons, of wallpaper fame, Thurbers, from Detroit, and others traveled to the shores of Minnicog.

In 1910 two large steel tanks, one with a capacity of 5000 gallons and the other of 8000 gallons, were erected on the side hill for water storage. The tanks were brought from Penetanguishene on a barge towed by a steam tug. It took three weeks to move them from the waters edge to their resting place. They were manipulated all the way on skids, pulled by block and tackle. After the tanks were in position a house was built around them and stained dark green. While that was being done miles of pipe were laid across the rocks and connected into the many buildings. A pump house was built on the south shore to shelter pump engines that drew water from the bay.

The north dock was eventually abandoned. A new dock was built in a fine harbour on the eastern side of the island in front of the main building, with smooth rock all the way to its door.

The passenger boats went up the outside channel between Minnicog and Smooth Island, around the north end of the island and maneuvered through the channel into the dock between a flat shoal barely covered with water and John's Island. When the ship was alongside and the lines secure the passengers disembarked and their luggage was hauled up the hill in a horse drawn cart.

A building only thirty feet from the main house held the bar and was one of the busiest places on the island until prohibition in 1916. This building also contained billiard tables and a barber shop. During this period of the First World War a number of causalities of that war were put up at Minnicog to convalesce.

Minnicog reached the peak of its glory as a summer resort after World War I. Miss Violet Pollard, the housekeeper, recalled many memories of the people who came there for their vacation. Cottagers from other islands came for dinner in the hotel dining room which had been added to the back of the main house and could seat 200 guests. Mr. Orville Wright who, with his brother Wilbur, invented and flew the first airplane, was a frequent dinner guest at Minnicog. He eventually built a cottage on Lambert Island, directly across the channel to the northeast from Minnicognashene.

The tables in the dining room were covered with white linen table cloths. Linen napkins folded to resemble a crown sat beside each place setting of sparkling silver and crystal. Twelve waitresses dressed in black uniforms and white caps and aprons looked after the tables. On Sundays they wore white uniforms. The kitchen was ruled by a chef with a tall, pleated hat on his head. He managed the meal planning and cooking with the aid of kitchen help. A pastry chef produced wonderful desserts.

A special nursery and dining room were provided for the children and their nurse maids so the parents could enjoy the dinner hour in the main dining room. Bellhops carried meals on large covered trays to those guests in the cottages who did not want to go to the dining room.

Evening entertainment was provided in the dance hall adjacent to the main building. The building was octagonal in shape with a cone shaped roof. The floor was smooth and there was a verandah around all eight sides of the hall. An orchestra was kept especially for the guest's pleasure and played each evening. A wood decked tennis court provided further entertainment possibilities and bowling was played on the front lawn. And every Sunday morning the Octagon building was used for church service.

The island was well lighted by acetylene gas from a large acetylene plant. There were light fixtures in every room and street lights were installed in the rocks so the guests could see their way to their cottages. The story is told that the night watchman made good money in tips from the guests he took home in a wheelbarrow after they had over-indulged at the bar.

It was not unusual to bump into a cow on the way to a cottage in the night. Cows were kept on the island during the summer months to supply milk for the hotel and for tourists on the surrounding islands who would row or paddle to Minnicog daily for their milk supply. The cows roamed all over the island and would have to be rounded up at milking time. Pigs were also kept in the barnyard as well as a horse to pull the luggage and supplies from the dock. There were chickens for fresh eggs and ducks and geese squabbled until it was time to kill them off to be dressed, cooked and served as a scrumptious dinner for the many guests.

The Minnicog Hotel was beautiful. Every part of it was spotless. There was one of the finest sand beaches for the swimmers. Flowers bloomed in front of the main house and along the pathways to each cottage. Flags flew from the tall flag pole and the air was crystal clear.

It took many people to operate the large hotel. Beside the dining room and kitchen staff there were the nursemaids, baggage men who delivered not only trunks and suitcases to the rooms, but also ice each morning to the cottages. Cliff Paradis, who later became lightkeeper at Brébuef Ranges, recalled getting a five cent tip from one lady who occupied the Big Ark. There were men to look after the maintenance of the lights and water. A man was needed to tend the vegetable garden and the stable that held from six to eight milking cows. There were very few motor boats at that time therefore guides, usually men from nearby Honey Harbour, would row the fishermen in row boats, until they had caught their catch for the day. Female staff were also needed to clean and make up the bedrooms. Summer romances occurred amongst the hired help even though the management set up strict rules against the men and women on staff fraternizing.

The women came from as far away as Toronto. The immigrants of that time were mainly Irish and English and were happy to get work. The Paradis brothers, Charlie and Clifford from Honey Harbour, met their wives at Minnicog. One girl over from England, the other from Ireland to make their way in the New World, found their destiny on an island in Georgian Bay. Clifford married the Irish girl, Mary, who was to become my lifelong friend. The France brothers from the nearby Freddy Channel were in charge of the boat house during the hotel days and one of those brothers, Wilfred met his future wife, Winnie, at Minnicog.

Although the rules were strict, the staff had their enjoyable times. They had a dance hall of their own close by the water. There was always someone amongst them who could play the violin and another who could call for the square dances which were so popular. Most of them were young and carefree. They could dance the night away after working a twelve hour day. Once during each summer season they were allowed to use the guest's dance hall. It was a gala affair and they dressed in their best for the occasion. For one special evening they danced to the music of an orchestra.

The Great Depression sounded the death knell to Minnicognashene's grandeur. Even though it remained the same grand place for several seasons and the tourists from neighbouring islands still came to dinner, the profits were down. The glory of the famed hotel began to decline. Buildings started to deteriorate, cream paint peeled from the exterior, roofs started to leak. The passenger boats stopped calling at the dock. By 1936 the fleet of boats, sailing dinghies, row boats and fishing boats had gone to rot. The enterprise closed down.

There was an attempt to purchase the island that year. The prospective buyer walked out on the ice from Penetanguishene with two men from a salvage company to look the place over. If the purchase had closed, the buildings would have been torn down and equipment hauled away. But Minnicog was saved for greater things.

In 1938 the island was purchased by Minnicog Limited, formed by a group of people who had been going to Minnicog for years. Some of them had purchased islands in the area. They bought the island from the Trust Company and formed the Minnicog Yacht Club. The buildings and docks were repaired and it became a private summer resort, remaining moderately active for a few years. But when war clouds loomed over Europe, gasoline was rationed, motor boats were laid up, many men from the club went into uniform, the Club went broke and the venture was forsaken. On May 29, 1941, the island was granted to Herbert C. Jarvis, a summer resident, for $1.00 - Etc.

There were still great things in store for Minnicognashene, completely different from anything it had known before. It was destined to become the largest Royal Canadian Sea Cadet Camp in Canada, playing host to thousands of cadets and naval personnel from across Canada and half way around the world. It was destined to have royalty, a

Governor General and Admirals walk upon its smooth, pink granite surface.

Gordon C. Leitch of Toronto, President of The Navy League of Canada, was the fairy godfather that rescued Minnicog from oblivion. He and his business associate, James Norris of Chicago, were cruising the waters around Minnicog. They, like so many before them, looked at the smooth rocks, the fine harbour, the large buildings and the wide sand beach. They decided it would make a perfect cadet camp, a sister Camp to the one that had been built on the northern tip of Beausoleil Island the previous year. On May 4, 1943, The Navy League of Canada acquired Minnicog Island, subject to restrictions, for $1.00 -Etc.

The main building of the Queen Elizabeth Camp on Beausoleil Island had been built in the shape of a ship's bridge. The building housed the administrative offices, mess hall and kitchens. The cadets were billeted in sleeping cabins built behind the main building. Boys ranging in age from fourteen to eighteen years of age were learning the skills of good seamanship on the waters of Georgian Bay.

The Queen Elizabeth Sea Cadet Camp on Beausoleil Island was small. When the two men, Leitch and Norris, donated Minnicog to the Navy League, contractors moved in to convert the old summer hotel into accommodation to serve the thousands of cadets that would use it as a training centre during the summer months.

The main house became the Administration building, its dining room became the mess hall. The kitchen was equipped with steam tables and modern cooking facilities and became the galley. The officers mess was in the main lounge and upstairs the officers had their rooms and offices. From his quarters in the southeast corner, the Commanding Officer could look out at the white ensign flying from the masthead and down to the dock where the ships were moored. There were many men from different parts of the country whose destiny was to command the Camp over the years.

The Bos'n Stores was set up in a square building some thirty feet from the administration building. The building that was once the staff dining room became the storehouse where everything from paint to rope, life jackets, soap and tools were kept with an officer in charge to sign out anything that was taken from stores.

The partitions in the large Annexes were ripped out and they were made into barracks for the cadets. At first, hammocks were slung across the long rooms but they were later replaced by steel bunk beds. The Winter House, our home, was the barracks for the Cadet Officers and the Green Cottage became a guest house for visiting dignitaries such as Vice Admiral Reed from Ottawa and Commanders from England, New Zealand and Australia. A Sick Bay was established in the famous bar close to the Administrative Building.

Meanwhile, arrangements were made to transport the cadets to the Camp aboard the ships the *Midland City* and the *City of Dover*.

Mr. J. Handly Smith, a scholarly gentleman from Toronto, was the civilian representative of The Navy League. Mr. Smith was also in charge of the Guest House.

All furnishings, equipment and administration of the Camp were under the Department of National Defence, Naval Services. Even the filling of the ice houses were under instructions from the Commanding Officer of H.M.C.S. York in Toronto.

In August of 1943 Princess Alice, wife of the Governor General, the Earl of Athlone and great aunt of Queen Elizabeth, arrived amidst great pomp and ceremony to christen the newly opened camp. From that day to the end of its years as a training camp, the Camp on Minnicog was known as the Princess Alice Sea Cadet Camp.

4

From Houseboat
to
Winter House

The fall weather was beautiful as we prepared to move into the Winter House, called that because it was the only building on the island warm enough to live in during the winter months. It was old fashioned with high ceilings and no insulation. But there was the north wall of cement and stone and the inside walls were lathe and plaster.

A fireplace was at one end of the living room and on chilly fall evenings kept us warm. But, as anyone who lives on the shore knows, it would be of no use in the winter. One of the first things to come up the hill from the houseboat was the wood burning cook stove. Frank hurriedly made a stone boat[6.] out of a couple of crooked tree trunks and some planks, hitched the horse to it and coaxed him out onto the dock.

We wiggled the white enameled kitchen range off the scow and onto the stone boat. The horse was young and skittish. When Frank said "get up" the horse just pranced and danced on the dock as soon as he felt the weight of the load on his collar.

Frank had a few choice words for the horse before he finally threw the leather lines down in disgust. I stood back and kept quiet. He unbuttoned his blue checked shirt, took it off and approached the horse. Billy tossed his head and

---

6. A stone boat is a sled-like vehicle made low to the ground, with runners, for hauling, among other things, stones when clearing land. Made from logs about six inches in diameter and, depending on the purpose of the boat, about four to six feet long. The long runners were chisled in front to round them up so that they would not catch on the rocks. Planks, three feet long were then nailed to the logs making the sled or stone boat complete.

Frank took hold of the bridle. He used his shirt for a blind-fold, and, after telling me to keep an eye on the stove, he led the horse off the dock.

Slowly the stove was pulled up the hill with the children and me trailing behind. My heart jumped every time the stone boat lurched over a crevice in the rocks. By the time we reached the back door I was starting to understand just what life on the island was going to be like.

By the time we had moved the stove through the back shed and into the kitchen my back was aching and my hands were blistered. There was great commotion as Frank put the tin stove pipes together, found an elbow to go into the chimney which we hoped wasn't blocked from above. Quickly he gathered kindling wood, a piece of paper and started a fire. Thankfully, the chimney was clear and the smoke went up the chimney and not into the room.

The autumn weather remained warm and sunny as we settled into our home. The Bay was quiet, the surface like a great mirror reflecting the glorious colours of the trees and the aqua sky. The air was mellow. Each evening the setting sun painted the water deep orange as it dipped down behind the Giant's Tomb.

The trees were dressed in their finest. The pale yellow of poplars, flaming reds and orange of maples and browns and burgundy of oak trees stood out in a brilliant display against the dark green of evergreens.

Bluejays called from the sumacs and partridge fed on bittersweet, the red berry growing on bushes in the swamps. Gulls swooped over the Bay and a pair of loons moved silently along the shore.

I liked the Winter House because it stood high up on the side hill. Through the French doors opening onto the verandah I had a splendid view of the island dotted waters. Boats from farther up the shore passed in front of the island on their way to town which was either Midland or Penetanguishene many miles away.

40 The Rourke family; first year at Minnicog

(Picture by Lorne Watson)

I stood and watched boats from Honey Harbour (a small tourist community on the mainland to the east of us) emerge through Tomahawk Channel. I knew the exact time to put the kettle on for lunch when Frank was working at the Queen Elizabeth Camp on the tip of Beausoleil because I could see the boat *Minnicog* as soon as it pulled out from the dock. The sound of the *Buchanan* motor in the boat became so familiar I could tell on a quiet day when he was leaving the dock in Midland twelve miles away.

It was a busy time for both of us. Frank had to make sure both Camps were laid up properly for the winter. There was a mile of water pipe to disconnect. Armed with wrenches he took them apart at the couplings to drain the water out so they would not freeze and burst during the winter. The many buildings had to be closed up and locked, coal to be hauled from Queen Elizabeth Camp to Minnicog by scow so we would have sufficient fuel to heat the house during the winter months.

It was too costly to operate the generating plant after the Camp was closed so I unpacked the kerosene lamps. There was an Aladdin lamp with its fragile mantle for the living room and various others with their fat bowls for the kitchen and bedrooms. I washed them in warm, soapy water, polished them until they gleamed and set them in a row on a bench in the back shed. I filled them with kerosene from a two-gallon can with a spout, wiped them off and they were ready when darkness came.

The Winter House had a living room, dining room, kitchen and bedroom on the lower floor. A sizeable pantry was tucked beneath the stairway. There were four bedrooms and a large bathroom upstairs. I realized the bathroom would be of no use in the winter since the island was rock and there was no way to bury the pipes. When the weather turned cold enough to freeze, Frank would have to drain the water from the huge tanks housed in the green building farther up the side hill. From then on the water would be carried from the lake by the pail full and our toilet facilities would be a little outhouse half hidden from view in a clump of trees thirty feet from the back door.

When I had an hour or so to spare I indulged in my favorite pastime of walking. I was anxious to explore every part of the island. I would tuck Bonnie in the carriage because the rocks were smooth enough to push it on.

I soon discovered our walks were not going to be peaceful. Billy, the horse, terrorized us whenever we stepped out the door. The baby carriage fascinated him. He could be down near the shore grazing or on the Parade Square munching peacefully on the grass and, the moment he saw us, he would take off on the gallop after us, tail up over his back. He would push his face in the carriage and nuzzle the baby while Gail and Gary clung to my legs screaming.

Soon I started playing a cat and mouse game with him. When we were ready to go out for an afternoon walk, I would look around to see where he was. If he was down near the shore we would sneak out the back door. If he was at the back of the Camp we would go out the front. I cautioned the little ones to be very quiet. Regardless of the precautions Billy would sense we were outside and come racing over the rocks to corner us.

I was never sure what he would be up to next. One afternoon, when I had finished the weekly laundry and hung it on a line Frank had strung up on the verandah, I did the usual checking on his whereabouts.

Billy was nowhere in sight. We walked to the Administration building where Frank was working and spent an enjoyable hour exploring. It was a big dwelling with many rooms both down and up. There were long corridors for the children to run along. From the windows on the third floor there was an incredible view of the surrounding waters. The chain of islands offered a scene of beauty and a sense of solitude.

There wasn't any sign of Billy when we started back to the house. It was most unusual and I thought he might have headed back into the centre of the island.

"I hope he stays there," I said to the children.

He wasn't of course. We were within twenty feet of the house when I saw him. He was on the verandah chomping on the clothes strung on the line. One of Frank's grey woolen socks was wrapped around his neck. The baby's little white undershirt was halfway down his throat.

It was a comical sight but I was really fed up with this horse who had antagonized me since the day we arrived at the island. I pushed the children into the house and grabbed the broom. Flinging the door leading to the verandah open I yelled at him.

"Get out of here!" I shouted, shaking the broom in his face. "Go away!"

Billy looked at me with innocent, brown eyes and kept on chewing the shirt.

"Back up!" I hollered, shaking the broom at him. He refused and I had the feeling the horse was laughing at me. I threw down the broom in exasperation and grabbed him by the metal ring in his halter.

He tossed his head while I attempted to unwind the sock from around his neck. I cringed as I pulled the slimy green shirt from his throat. He refused to back out of the door so I coaxed him to turn around and led him off the verandah.

I was still fuming when Frank came in for supper. His eyes danced with amusement while I ranted and raved. When supper was over, he went quietly down the hill to the workshop with Billy clip-clopping behind him. Frank stopped to pat his neck and the horse nipped playfully at the sleeve of his shirt.

Within an hour there was a gate across the doorway on the verandah that put an end to the horse feasting on the laundry. It wasn't the end of his pranks by any means. He kept my attempts at outdoor activities in constant turmoil until it was time to tie him in the barn for the winter.

Billy was a playboy and the idea of work was beyond his comprehension. It had taken over an hour to get him to pull the cookstove up to the house. When Frank hitched him to the stone boat to haul the coal from the shore to the storage shed back of the house, Billy refused to budge. The moment he felt the weight of the load on his collar he would slacken off and turn his head to look at Frank.

It was Frank's turn to be provoked with the horse. He dropped the leather lines and grabbed him by the halter. Billy reared up on his hind legs. Before the coal was in storage for the winter both man and beast had to give a little. Frank lightened the load by half and the horse finally gave in to the inevitable.

We parted with Billy as soon as the ice was thick enough to take him to town. When he saw his first car it was Billy's turn to be terrorized. The shore horse had never seen such a contraption before and he tore down the road after it at full gallop. Frank pulled on the reins and hollered for half a mile before he could get the frightened runaway horse under control. When he got him tied in the livery stable he contacted a horse dealer and traded him for an old work horse named Tom. I have often thought about Billy and wondered if he finally realized he was a horse instead of a person.

We had been working so hard the first few weeks neither Frank nor I gave any thought to the fact we had no visitors to the island. For one thing, we had not become acquainted with our neighbors. Actually, there were several miles of water and numerous islands between us and the other year 'round residents. There wasn't a light to be seen when we looked out at night. Being reared on the shore, we were both content with life the way it was.

Our first visitors came on a mellow October day. The children and I had just returned from a walk over the rocks down into the bush skirting the edge of a marsh where the tall grass had been bleached from green to a tawny straw colour. We kicked the first fallen leaves as we pushed our way through a tangle of blackberry bushes that grabbed at our clothing. We stepped over rotting logs covered with soft green moss and pushed aside prickly juniper bushes.

The afternoon air was crisp and clear. The north wind had a slight nip to it. The sky was brilliant blue. The golden sun filtered down through the trees, playing on the bright colour of the leaves. Every tree was a different tint. Oak trees varied in shades of brown to tan to deepest burgundy. Maple trees displayed dresses of red and flamboyant orange. The soft maples and poplars were a shimmering yellow. The dark green of white pine and lacy red cedar made a dramatic background.

At the far end of the marsh a flock of Bluejays flitted in and out of the woods, their blue and white wings flashing as they called out a warning that we were invading their forest home.

A partridge startled us as it shot out of a clump of bittersweet, its swift wings drumming the air. Every hollow tree seemed to be the home of a chipmunk or squirrel and we were loudly scolded as we passed by.

We wandered idly through the woods until we came to the westward side of the island. There the wide expanse of Georgian Bay lay before us dancing joyfully under the autumn sun. Out across the restless waters the Giant's Tomb was wrapped in a soft purple haze. Farther out I could distinguish the Pine Islands and the Watchers.

We were back to the house and I was bathing the baby when a small boat stopped at the dock. For a few minutes I was flustered. The house was not as it should be yet, strangers were coming and I was caught with a baby in a bath tub.

When Clifford and Mary Paradis walked through the door that golden day in October we did not realize it then but the lightkeeper from Brébeuf Ranges and his wife had walked into our lives forever. From that day on we shared adventure, joy and even heartaches. Mary and Cliff were destined to become a second set of parents to our children.

Frank had spoken to me about the Paradis' when we passed in front of the lighthouse that stood a half mile off the shore of Beausoleil Island. The lighthouse with a dwelling attached was known as the Head Light and was situated on Brébeuf Island which was small with smooth rocks and partially wooded. The Tail Light was situated directly behind it, a quarter of a mile across rocky, shoal infested waters on the westward side of Beausoleil Island. The Tail Light was a square, steel skeleton type tower surmounted by a white watch room. These lights, in line, guide the vessels from the Giant's Tomb to the ports of Midland and Port McNicoll.

The Paradis' were well acquainted with Minnicognashene. They first met on the island when Mary, fresh out from County Tyrone Ireland, was a dining room girl at the hotel. Cliff, from Honey Harbour, was a part time guide and Bell Hop and did what ever else there was to do at the hotel requiring a strong young man. They met in the summer, married in September. Mary forgot about going on to the United States, her intention when she left Ireland. From then on it was life on the shore, traveling by dog team in winter to visit relatives in Go Home Bay and Honey Harbour. Summer was spent working with the tourist industry until they took up lightkeeping in 1931.

That day in 1943 was the beginning of an extraordinary friendship that made my life and that of my family richer.

There was much to do from the time we arrived at Minnicog until freeze up. We would be isolated for several weeks or even a month or so. We had to get bulk provisions put in to see us through the winter. It was an exciting situation all along the island strewn shore at that time. People at the north end of the shore went to Parry Sound, a twenty-eight-mile trip for some, to get their supplies. The gas boat *Shuffle Along* made the run down as far as Moon River, loaded with baled hay, oats and other big articles. The

Geraldine, out of Penetanguishene, hauled supplies to Wah Wah Taysee.

Almost every fair weather day a boat went by the island, steam curling from the exhausts, with folks intent on getting their supplies in before the ice formed. Christmas had to be considered. Santa was expected to call, even up the shore.

The children nearly wore out the Christmas mail order catalogue. They were fascinated by dolls, trucks, teddy bears and Lone Ranger and Roy Rogers cap guns.

"Look Mummy, this is what I want for Christmas!" they would exclaim.

I made a mental note of whatever was wanted. Later I listed it on the order form which, at that time, was in the back of the catalogue. The order was posted no later than the last week in October.

Just as important was the list of groceries we needed to carry us through most of the winter. I kept a list handy and, whenever I thought of something, I marked it down. If I forgot something we did without until the Bay froze hard enough to travel on.

We bought in large quantities. Flour by the 100 lb. bag, four at least since we would have men in the winter to help fill the two large ice houses. White sugar by the 100 lb., brown sugar by 50 lb., tea, cornstarch, salt, syrup in five pound pails, canned milk by the forty-eight can case since there was no fresh milk supply. So many items to remember. Coffee was a very important item because Frank thought breakfast without coffee was no breakfast at all.

We brought the load of staple goods in by the second week in October. Frank took the list down to the store a week ahead of time. It was ready to be loaded into the delivery truck and taken to the dock as soon as they knew we were in town. Frank chose a day when the wind was in the south and the sun was shining to go for the load. We wanted to get it home and under shelter without getting it wet. When the boat was tied to our dock, the work began. Even the children helped to bring the big load up to the house. Before nightfall the pantry and the kitchen were stacked with boxes and bags. We sat down exhausted to a make-shift supper.

The next morning I started the big chore of storing the supplies away on the shelves of the pantry underneath the stairway. Some of the shelves were already filled with pickles and Chili Sauce, pears, peaches and plums I had canned earlier in the season. It took me the better part of two days to rip open the cases and pile everything neatly in rows. Frank emptied the sugar and one bag of flour into hundred pound tins. The rest of the flour was stood against the wall. Split peas for soup, white beans and rice were stored in tin cans, usually empty five pound baking powder cans. I also had a row of gallon pickle jars that were handy for that purpose.

A second list was ready for the first part of November. We waited as long as we could for the order of fresh meat and vegetables because they were hard to keep. We had to go spare on fresh meat such as beef and pork until the temperature was cold enough to keep it frozen in the back shed. In the early part of winter we relied on salt pork, breakfast bacon by the side, bologna by the roll and canned meats. Eggs were bought in a thirty dozen carton, potatoes by the seventy-pound bag, Spy apples by the barrel and oranges by the wooden crate. A twenty-five-pound bag of cooking onions also found its place in the bulging pantry.

The horse had to be remembered on the shopping list. Frank took care of that part of the supplies. Baled hay came in by the ton and oats by the bag to be stored in the barn down by the boat house.

I will never forget one year. During the last trip before winter set in, ice started to form on Midland harbour while I was uptown racing from store to store. Last minute shopping entailed a lot of purchasing: warm footwear for the children, parcels to pick up at the mail order offices, Christmas gift buying to do and, always, boxes of groceries.

I had progressed downtown from one store to another when Glen, who was nine by then, found me. He was out of breath and pretty agitated.

"Daddy said to hurry up!" said Glen. "We have to get going because its starting to freeze at the dock."

"Hurry!" I nearly collapsed. That is just what I had been doing for two hours. The folks in the shoe store, knowing us well, co-operated by hurriedly wrapping up the fleece lined rubbers and adding them to already over burdened arms.

I followed my son down the last two blocks. We crossed the railway tracks at high speed. My lungs were protesting and so were my arms. The boat was untied by the time I got to the *Midland Boat Works.* Over the side the parcels and I fell and we were under way, ice closing in behind us as we made for the safety of our island home.

5

Fall Freeze-Up

The onslaught of winter made it necessary to shut down the gas driven water pump. Water pipes were disconnected and drained.

Our water came from the bay during the long cold months, from a hole chopped through the ice near the shore. The water was carried to the house in fourteen quart galvanized pails, a tedious, daily chore up the snow covered hill in all kinds of weather. The little ones helped, carrying the water in five pound honey cans with wire handles Frank had attached to the pails.

Water was emptied into the reservoir on the wood burning cook stove which supplied the warm water for washing dishes, faces and hands. Dish pans and wash basins were part of our way of life in the winter months.

The tea kettle sang on top of the cook stove. The tea pot sat on one of the back lids. What a wonderful comfort our cook stove supplied. It made the kitchen cosy, baked bread, cookies, roasts and chickens. When my feet were cold I would open the oven door, pull up the rocking chair and toast my toes in the heavenly heat.

With the water shut off there was none to flush the toilet in the bathroom upstairs. Now our toilet was a "two holer" about thirty feet from the back door with no heat and no lights. We lit a kerosene lantern to find our way after dark. I soon realized why there were so many chamber pots at Minnicog!

Freeze-up also meant it was getting close to Christmas.

Getting the Christmas tree was a delightful afternoon spent in the woods. Frank sharpened his axe, took the horse from his winter stable and hitched him to the sleigh. Away we went, up over the hill, past the great building on the summit, through the frosty snow to the Christmas tree marsh.

The younger ones hopped off the sleigh to follow the hard packed rabbit trails while we looked for our special tree. We floundered in the snow from one end of the marsh to the other. It was beautiful, surrounded by snow covered evergreens. Oh the smell, the silence.

After much debating Frank made the final choice. The axe bit into the trunk, the sound echoing through the bush. With a flurry of snow the tree toppled to the ground. The boys pulled it out to where the horse was waiting and loaded it onto the sleigh. We scrambled on and were off for home, trace-chains jangling.

There was great happiness setting it up in the corner of the living room after the lamps were lit and darkness shrouded the Bay.

With Christmas fast approaching, we watched the Bay like a cat watches a mouse. Without refrigeration we had to leave the shopping for the "bird" until just before Christmas Day. The turkey was a big part of our Christmas.

We were filled with glee when the Bay froze over. But gloom settled over us when a nor'wester roared in over Giant's Tomb and smashed it. Time and again it happened. Finally, one crisp, starlit night Frank came in from the barn and said he figured by morning the ice would be thick enough to walk on.

Next morning he slipped his arms through the straps of his knapsack. Taking with him a long handled ice chisel to test the ice, he made his way across the new ice to Payette's Island. He walked across Beausoleil Island and crossed over to Honey Harbour where he hired a taxi to take him to Midland.

Late in the afternoon the children and I watched anxiously, looking eastward, until we saw Frank walk onto the ice at Payette's Island. Oh, the excitement! He had made it! The boys ran to the shore to meet him.

They escorted him into the house where he wiggled out of the shoulder straps dropping the heavy load to the floor. The fun of opening it up! Out came the turkey wrapped in brown butcher's paper, the Christmas parcel from Mother and Father Myers, stacks of cards and letters. After supper and the dishes washed, a contented family settled down to listen to Christmas carols over the battery operated radio and read our mail.

Happiness filled the house on Christmas eve. The joy and wonder were reflected in the blue eyes of our children.

Then came the rush of Christmas morning with children creeping downstairs amid excited whispering. Four stockings were hung on the red brick fireplace. Glen carried Bonnie, the babe, carefully downstairs. Gary and Gail followed close behind. When they could contain themselves no longer they were all in our bed greeting us with sticky kisses.

We were pulled out of bed. The cook stove was lit. Within half an hour we were wading knee deep in wrapping paper. There were new sweaters and pajamas from Nanna and Gramps. Pretty dolls and toy trucks. A pop gun for Gary and a Roy Rogers pistol for Glen and a toboggan for all. The side hill was snow covered. After an early dinner the toboggan was taken outside where three happy youngsters climbed the hill. Glen, our eldest gave a shove and off they raced, sliding and jumping until they careened out onto the bay.

They brought the toboggan back up, squabbling a bit about who should do the pulling. Once on top they went frolicking back down, their happy laughter making a merry sound.

When they grew older and increased in number by two, they became skilled at maneuvering the downward run. They stood like soldiers, hands resting on each other's shoulders. With a gentle kick they started to slide, wind tugging at their pant legs, whipping their hair, tinting their cheeks rosy red. Down the hill they went on wings of pure joy like birds in flight.

Bakelite serving trays eventually became the favourite slider. The slightest slope and the shiny surfaced trays moved easily. The children and I wandered many places sitting on the trays. Maneuvering with our hands we crossed the island or plunged at break neck speed down our favourite slope onto the frozen Minnicog bay.

Our first New Years came on a sparkling winters night, the Big Dipper and the North Star brilliant in the northern sky. With the old year drawing to a close we gathered in the living room. When the clock struck twelve, we leaped up, kissed and hugged, wishing one another "Happy new year!" I poured tea into cups set up on the table, a table spread with the good food of the season. This was a tradition handed down from my Scottish ancestors ensuring we would have plenty of food on the table for the next twelve months.

We watched New Years morning wondering if we would have a "first foot"[7] and who it would be. A dark haired man is preferred. He is supposed to bring the best luck of all for the coming year. The "first foot" must never come empty handed. If they carried no gift they were dispatched to the wood pile to carry in a few sticks, a symbol that there would be plenty of everything, food, clothing and good luck all year through. The Irishman in my life went along with the yearly ritual.

Brother-in-law Emery was our "first foot". He had walked many miles across the ice to see for himself that all was well with us and to give us news of family and friends. The contents of his knapsack was enough to keep up the old tradition but he carried in some extra wood from the wood pile just to make sure the luck was with us. Emery was a perfect "first foot".

---

[7]. The First Foot is a Scottish tradition probably dating from the time of the Norse invasions some centuries ago. These Norsemen were fair haired.

64 Right to Left: Glen, Gail, Gary, Bonnie Gaye, Garnet, Gillard

39 Emery O'Rourke

6

Filling the Ice Houses

Once freeze-up was complete, when the ice on the Bay was sixteen to eighteen inches thick, it was time to prepare for harvesting the ice. We had to put up three hundred tons of ice in the huge old grey ice house at Minnicog. One hundred tons would be stored in the ice house at Queen Elizabeth Camp on the northern tip of Beausoleil Island also.

We arranged with Frank's brother Emery, who lived in Cognashene (an area of the shore a few miles from Minnicog), to help fill the ice houses. He came with his team of horses and his workmen.

The quiet days were over. We were up at quarter to six in the morning. The lids on the cook stove rattled as we built the fire. The tea kettle was brought to a boil while the men headed for the barn carrying a lantern in the morning darkness to water, feed and harness the horses.

I made hot cereal, fried bacon and eggs. I watched the toast didn't burn on the wire rack on top of the stove. The men came in from the barn, swept the snow off their leather topped rubber boots and washed up at the hand basin on a bench beside the back door. They gathered around the table in the dining room.

The men were out of the house by seven thirty, leading the horses from the barn, hitching them to a set of sleighs, usually bob-sleighs with a wooden rack. Ice saws, with big teeth for sawing the ice, large ice tongs to haul the cakes out of the frigid water, chisels and axes were all put on the sleighs. The teamster picked up the long leather reins, said "get up!" to the horses standing ready to pull the sleighs to the shore and they were off with a lurch. Often snow had to be scraped off the ice. The ice was scored off in squares reminding me of how I marked off squares of a cake, only much larger.

It wasn't easy work out on the wind swept Bay. There were special jobs for each man. There was a knack to cutting and storing of ice so it would keep during the hot weather.

The cutting started with the "T" block being cut out first. The sawyer followed the lines with his ice-saw while another man blocked off, which meant he cut the long strip into blocks, straight and true so they would fit together in the ice house. It was almost a work of art and not everyone made a good sawyer.

Frank usually hired the same men year after year, knowing who was the most capable for the job. The Dusome boys, Narfield and Leonard from Highland Point, George Corbier and James and Eddie Lizotte from Honey Harbour were some of the men.

When the first blocks were floating in the dark water they were grabbed with ice tongs and hauled out on the ice. The blocks were lifted from the ice onto the sleighs. If there was enough snow on the road to the ice house it was possible to load sixteen to twenty heavy, sparkling blue cakes on one load. The men worked all day with water sloshing around their rubber boots.

There was a high mound of saw dust in front of the ice house door. Usually it was thrown out in the fall before it became frozen in the ice house. The horses pulled hard on their collars as they drew the heavy load up onto the saw dust pile.

9 Charlie Cascanette & Charlie Myers

10 Hauling ice cakes

"Whoa there," the teamster would say to the perspiring horses. The cakes were quickly unloaded, passed to the packer, the only man to spend the day in some sort of shelter. He was a craftsman too since the blocks had to fit neatly together, layer after layer with snow packed between them and a layer of saw dust over top.

When they were storing the ice at Minnicog the men came in at noon for their meal, a hearty meal of soup, potatoes, meat, vegetables and pie for dessert. One o'clock saw everyone swing back into action.

The work crew at Queen Elizabeth Camp on Beausoleil carried a packed lunch, not sandwiches, but a good hearty meal. They used tin plates and enamel cups, as well as a blackened pail made from a large tin can with a wire handle for boiling the tea. The pail got blackened from the open fire. They carried hay for the horses at their mid-day break with a bag of oats thrown in. At noon a fire was built on the ice at the shore. The tea pail was filled from the ice hole and hung over the fire to boil. It was often said the tea was strong enough to float a four inch nail.

When the sun slanted west ward and the chill of late day crept in, brush was placed at each corner of the open hole, markers to show there was danger. The tools and lunch box were loaded on the sleighs. The ice house door was closed. The ice harvesters headed home for a hot supper and a rest before going out again the next morning, unless a blizzard storming across the Bay kept them off the ice.

There were ice houses at all cottages and cabins. Some took several days to fill, some only a day, depending on the size.

The harvest went on up and down the shore, from Penetanguishene (in front of the military establishment for the "Insane Asylum"), Midland (the Pratt company) and northward to Go Home Bay, Wah Wah Taysee, Sans Souci and on to Parry Sound.

This was a time before hydro[8], before refrigeration on the shore and filling ice houses was a way of making extra money for those living along the island chain.

Towards spring, when the sawdust piles in front of the ice houses thawed, the sawdust was shovelled over the ice a foot or more deep to keep it from melting during the summer months.

---

[8]. Electricity

7

First Winter

When the ice-house filling was completed, it was a quiet time at my island home. The Paradis' had left the lighthouse at close of navigation. Winter travel was by horse and sleigh and "shore folk" travelled the outside channel, away from the narrows in front of Minnicog and other dangers of bad ice along the inside channel.

One of my greatest joys was looking eastward towards Beausoleil each morning to watch the great herd of deer (I counted as many as three hundred) make its way to the many small islands in the area to eat off the red cedar branches. Several deer, maybe six or eight, came within two hundred feet of our house, ever watchful but not really afraid when they helped themselves to the red cedar. They were graceful and beautiful, always alert to danger, ready to bound away if they became frightened.

The herd was well protected at that time as they are today on Beausoleil Island, a National Park. There was little to disturb them except a small pack of wolves and sometimes they were startled by the Warden patrolling the park. It was a wonderful era and I was fortunate to have been in a place where I could enjoy their coming and going each winter's day.

I made one trip to town by horse and cutter across Corbeau's Island and down the gap to Pinery Point. It seemed to take a long time to reach the Ontario Hospital (now called the Mental Health Centre) where we left the ice. By the time we were off Gin Rock my feet felt like two blocks of ice even though they were covered with heavy socks and warm boots. After a few miles the hay in the bottom of the sleigh and the heavy robe over my knees did not help.

Painfully I would leap from the sleigh and follow behind, walking in the runner tracks. The longer I dog-trotted the more I realized the horse was not going so slow after all. After fifteen minutes I was ready to jump back onto the sleigh.

In February, when the days grew longer, we had the urge to visit my parents in Moon River. Frank tacked canvas around the cutter as a wind break and covered the bottom with hay. I dressed the children in their warmest clothing and covered the house plants with newspaper so they wouldn't freeze in our absence. With a lunch basket packed full we departed Minnicog in the early morning.

Frank was an old hand at travelling the shore by horse. We took to the gap outside the islands and headed in the general direction of One Tree Island. He knew where the dangerous narrows were, knew when to try the ice with his axe and when to portage over the islands. Glen, Gail and Gary enjoyed the journey. When their feet were cold they jumped off the sleigh and raced alongside. Bonnie, nine months old, was content in a basket at my feet.

When Frank went ahead to try the ice I took the reins to the horse. Billy had been traded for Tom and he was definitely a woman hater. The moment I took the reins he slowed down. The farther Frank went ahead the slower the horse moved until he finally came to a stand still.

"Smack him with the reins," Frank would shout.

I smacked and Tom just turned his head to look back at me with scornful brown eyes but, eventually, we made it across Twelve Mile Bay. Dusk gathered as we made our way over the twisting road towards Moon river. The hills seemed more steep, the trees much closer after dark. Far off at the bottom of Twelve Mile Bay we heard the howls of a wolf pack. The journey seemed endless across the peninsula.

The lights at Arnold's house were a welcome sight. We dropped in at the familiar home of my distant cousins long enough to heat the baby's bottle, a short break before starting down river towards Woods Bay. We stopped at the Tessier's who had taken over the Sweet place near where Six Mile Creek drains into the Bay. We sat at a long table and ate heartily of home made bread and strawberry jam, shore hospitality at its best.

It was just past nine o'clock when we reached Father and Mother Myers home on Woods Bay. We sent Glen, our five year old, to rap on the door. I can still hear the exclamation of astonishment when the door was opened.

"Glen!" gasped Mother Myers, "How did you get here?"

The creaking of the horse's harness and the chatter of little people answered her question. It was a rare event to have her family arrive in the middle of winter, and how happy she was to have us. Winter or summer the greeting was always the same. Father Myers stoked up the fire while Mother Myers bustled around the kitchen. We settled down with feet towards the fire, tired but relaxed after a long trip.

After a couple of days of enjoying my folk's company, exchanging news of the shore, it was time for the homeward trek. We started early with the replenished lunch basket hidden away somewhere amongst the hay.

37 Trip to Moon River

Frank, and Juanita Rourke, Euphemia (Mother Myers)

We stopped for awhile to visit with Frank's sister, Gladys and her husband Johnny Martin who were in camp[9] at Tadnac.

We were fed and made welcome which is the way of the shore and we caught up on the happenings in the Wah Wah Taysee area.

---

9.   Working at a lumber camp.

Leaving there we made our way south past Bands Island and One Tree. I looked across the frozen water to see the Pine Islands and Giants Tomb standing bold against the blue of the sky. It was a fine day with the wind in the south.

The day was spent by the time we caught sight of the tall white chimneys of the main building at Minnicog. As we pulled into our yard the sun was gone and my teeth were chattering. Into the cold house we rushed to build fires in the stoves. It was mighty fine to be home, to take the newspaper off the plants and discover they were fine too. It was the last trip I made up the shore by horse and sleigh. The means of faster transportation was just a few years away.

8

Wolves Up The Shore

Dusk, that time of day when the ice and the mainland blend together minutes after the sun disappears below the western horizon, was the moment the grey wolf came loping across the white bay, skirting the open narrows and over the point of the island.

Time or route never varied. I could stand at the window and watch him coming from the mainland where he had spent the day. He ran low to the ice with his bushy tail floating out behind him.

He was a friendly fellow. That he craved human companionship was evident by the big paw marks we noticed around the house in the mornings after a light fall of snow. He spent one night curled up beside the verandah, moving off before daybreak to the hunting grounds across the bay.

He was bold enough only once to appear during the day. He was standing by the dock when we saw him. He was a tall rangy fellow. He was standing with one paw held up watching the house. His ears were up, every inch of his body was alert. He was getting too bold and we felt he was a potential danger to the children. Frank took a crack at him with the rifle.

The opening of the door had startled him and he was off across the ice, making great long jumps before Frank had the rifle to his shoulder. The bullet threw snow up at his heels as he raced away in terror. From then on he kept his distance and spent no more nights curled up beside our front door.

I have a real affection for the wild shaggy animal with his dignity and independence and there was no intention to harm the grey beast but we had to be sure he would not hurt our own. Like an old friend, I looked for him each winter evening, crossing the ice as dusk gathered across the Bay.

Wolves lurked along the shore long before the white man came. You will find the shaggy beast pouncing on the slow or the weak where game is thick They were numerous when grandfather Myers pioneered the shore. Their howls were one of the first things to make Mother Myers hair stand on end when she was fresh out from Scotland. Frank has hunted them in the moonlight with an Indian friend who became so apprehensive he lit birch bark torches to get a better view of the lake where the wolves were crouched.

The howls of a wolf pack on a cold clear winters night can be spine-chilling to the hardiest soul. It is an eerie, unearthly sound that sends chills up the back and raises the hair on the back of the neck. It always makes me want to scurry to the warmth and brightness of the house, any house, so long as it has four thick walls and a stout door. And I wonder why because never once has a wolf made any effort to come near. Wolves are easily frightened and will turn and run away when other animals will stand their ground. But still I get "spooky" every time I hear their mournful howl. They can make quite a chorus chasing a rabbit around a marsh or when in pursuit of a deer across an ice-covered lake.

A pack of wolves was after a deer one night that I remember most vividly. My brother and I were playing hockey in the moonlight. We had cleared a rink earlier in the day. We stood a lantern in the centre of the rink so we could keep track of the puck. A cold wind was whistling over the North Hill and the moon and stars were brilliant in the sky. The night was quiet, quiet as a night can be when the neighbors are few and far between. Despite the lantern, the puck became lost in the snow banks. I was poking around with my foot in search of it when the air was suddenly filled with the blood curdling howls of a wolf pack after game.

I fairly froze in my tracks. My brother Allie, at the other end of the rink, seemed to be a mile away and the lights of the house much farther. The terrifying noise seemed so close I expected to see the brutes come dashing out of the shadows at the shore.

I came to life suddenly. I leaped from the snow bank and landed sitting down on the ice. Wildly I scrambled to my feet and tore down the ice certain the whole pack was right at my heels.

"Wolves," I gasped coming up to my brother. "Be quiet," he hissed, moving over to pick up the lantern. "Let's go home and tell dad," he said, lifting up the lantern globe and blowing out the light.

"Yes, let's," I agreed, trying to match his long strides with my shorter legs, all the while glancing over my shoulder.

Once inside the door I closed it quickly behind me. The quiet house came alive. There was a click of guns as Father Myers and my brother loaded them. Coats were shrugged into and they slipped out the door.

I couldn't quite understand why they wanted to go out into the eerie darkness up over the hill where the evergreens grew thickly. But Mother Myers explained the reason.

It seemed the wolves were on Myers Lake, a mile back of the house. Since the moonlight made the outdoors almost as bright as day, it would be easy to see the dark figures of the wolves against the white surface of the lake.

I sat on the bottom step of the stairway biting my finger nails until I heard the crunch of their footsteps on the snow outside. I felt a warm glow when Father Myers stepped through the door, Allie behind him.

"We didn't get a shot at them," he said. "They were at the far end of the lake by the time we got up there."

"They were chasing a fair sized deer," he told us, as he hung his rifle on the rack. "The way the lake is churned up with tracks, I'd say the deer was giving them quite a run."

"Were there many wolves?" I asked my brother.

"Dad thinks there are seven in the pack," he told me. "He says the leader is a big old fellow and the deer won't have much chance once it gets into deep snow." I crept upstairs, and when I was ready for bed, I pulled the covers over my head.

I think it was the elusiveness of the wolf that frightened me, the fact he could melt into the shadows and be gone so quickly. If he wasn't so wary and cunning perhaps I could have understood him.

It was a warm day in hunting season when Mother Myers and I were alone that I discovered we were being watched very closely. On a high bald rock on the top of the north hill, a shaggy figure sat silhouetted against the sky. Only when he turned his sharp snout to the sky to let out a mournful cry did he take his eyes off our house. All day long he sat there, watching, unmoving, like a statue until four o'clock. We were keeping a wary eye on him. Then, suddenly, he disappeared down over the back of the hill and did not return.

Wolves still roam the swamps and hills up the shore and are very much a part of this magnificent land.

9

Spring Break-Up

March had gone out like a gentle lamb. The winds were light, the sun poured down its glory from an azure sky.

April came in as fresh as dew on a rose. With it came April showers. It pattered down steadily but gently all night, waking the creek, sending it rushing and tumbling down to the Bay. A joyous release from winter's grip.

The snow vanished. Our feet, clad in winter rubbers felt clumsy and leaden when we walked on the rocks. The children shed their rubber boots to run gleefully across the verandah and over the bare grey rocks.

The ice turned from a firm, white highway to a sodden, water soaked mass. The patches of water grew larger with each day.

Overnight hundreds of birds appeared. Starlings, blackbirds, sparrows and robins flitted everywhere. Even a blue heron flapped slowly overhead.

One rainy Wednesday, at noon, the black smoke of the first out going lake freighters could be seen rolling up over Midland Point.

While we stood in the rain, watching from the Rock Cottage hill for the first ships to round Midland Point, two men left Gendron's Channel to walk down past Brébeuf Lighthouse. Walking easily pulling a handsleigh, it was not until they reached Gin Rock were they aware of the freighters breaking their way out.

The men made a hasty journey across the gap to Pinery Point. They stopped to watch the ships cut a channel across where they had walked such a short while before.

The *Lemoyne* led the way. Built in 1926, the *Lemoyne* was the largest Laker for many years and flagship of the C.S.L. fleet. Progress was slow through heavy ice. Two more freighters followed in the wake of the *Lemoyne*. Behind them puffed the *Bayport*, the only ice breaker in our region at that time. She looked tiny midst miles of ice.

Sound carried well. The noise of the propellers churning and the crunch of ice against the bow of the ships could be heard clearly.

By mid afternoon the nose of the mighty *Coverdale* came out of the mist hanging over Midland Point. Quickly she passed the other ships taking her place ahead of the *Lemoyne*, a triumphant lead out through the ice bound Bay into the freedom of the outer lakes beyond.

More ships followed later until, at dusk, all that could be seen of the winter fleet were the billowing clouds of black smoke far out past Giant's Tomb.

Suddenly it happened! After months of being up to our necks in snow the melody of spring was all about us. Every inch of snow had melted from the hills, draining off in happy little streams towards the Bay.

The last bar of ice binding us in departed. It left as only ice on the broad sweep of the Bay can leave. With a strong east wind driving it relentlessly it disintegrated into a million particles. The swish of its breaking was music to our ears.

To the west, far out by Giant's Tomb, groups of white ice cakes drifted in from the outer Bay. Some drifted idly until they melted while others were caught on the ragged shoals, piled up like mushrooms and were attacked by the warm rains or brilliant sun.

11 *Bayport* breaking ice in Midland Harbour *(picture by Bev Keefe)*

35 Ship trapped in ice *(picture by Bev Keefe)*

It is wonderful to wake to the lilting song of the robin and the sweet low notes of the song sparrow; to rise and go softly to the window and watch the black ducks swimming near the dock and up towards the marsh where they have nested the past few years.

Our friends, the red headed duck and her mate who spent many summers at Minnicog, fished for their breakfast each morning just a stone's throw from the house. They came in close to shore, swimming easily amongst the weeds, racing with their heads under the water, feeding on the schools of minnows. Doubtless they were thinking about a summer home. One year it was near the Winter House. The year before, the Nimitz Block which stood a little higher up on the hill with the chimney towering above the tree tops. I kept watching the many houses which dot the island and wondered which one would be chosen that year. Surely, after such lofty castles, the old red head would never be satisfied with a more humble home.

The gulls fly high over head, white wings flashing as they circle the Bay searching for fish, screeching with a joy kin to madness when one of them would dart down like a streak of lightning and come up with a minnow clutched in its beak.

I remember the evenings being exquisitely beautiful. Soft rose and purple glistened against the inky black of the open water and frogs singing their hearts out in the marsh down by the boat house.

For at least one week each spring activities centered around our boat the *Minnicog*. Sandpaper smoothed the hull and a new color scheme covered the paint of another year.

When we launched her for another year she slipped into the Bay with a gentle splash. There is something wonderful in having the boats "back in" and to hear the motors coming to life after so many months of idleness.

The weekends held promise of much activity. Lights pop on in the surrounding cottages - cottages that stood empty and lifeless during the cold months. Friday night the folks would arrive from Paris, Ontario, Toronto and Buffalo. Familiar faces greeted us and familiar hands shook ours. The folks from the south were glad to be back, glad to see the grey rocks, the twisted pines and the Bay. Yes, and the most important thing of all, the only place in the world for us is Georgian Bay in the spring.

10

Navy Days

With the arrival of our first spring at Minnicog, our way of life changed dramatically. The days, the years ahead would prove to be exciting and challenging. A way of life few island dwellers would ever know.

The first Navy personnel arrived in May 1944 to inspect the Camp and to start preparations for the season ahead when the sea cadets would come aboard in late June.

The summer Camps of Queen Elizabeth on the northern tip of Beausoleil Island and Princess Alice Camp at Minnicognashene were operated by the Navy League of Canada in cooperation with Naval Services. They were among the best boys camps in Canada. The cadets were under direct supervision of their own officers who, in turn, worked with the help and cooperation of instructors of the Royal Canadian Navy Reserve.

Sailing, swimming and rowing were taught. Life belts were required when aboard any craft and, under the watchful eyes of an instructor, the cadets were permitted to steer, navigate and operate the boats.

There was much work to be done between May and the arrival of the Sea Cadets at the end of June. A tractor and small trailer were brought in to haul the material and goods brought to the island by the harbour crafts. Workmen were busy everywhere.

When Frank took over supervision of the work and maintenance, I took over the job of feeding the crew of men he hired. The crew could consist of as few as four or as many as twelve.

We were up in the morning at six o'clock, feeding the fire in the wood burning cookstove. I stirred oatmeal, toasted bread on a wire rack on top of the stove and fried bacon and eggs.

Each week I ordered two sides of bacon, sliced, from the butcher in Midland.

I did the baking after breakfast was over and the dishes cleared away. Making pies, cakes and home made bread were all part of a daily ritual. The men came in at noon, settling around the big table in the kitchen for a three course meal. Frank ate with them then disappeared into the living room for a twenty minute "siesta". Then he was off again until quitting time when, once again, I had a hearty three course meal waiting for the men. I especially remember how James Lizotte, one of the workmen and a fine man, enjoyed beef stew and dumplings.

In June, the chef and galley crew moved into the Camp. I gladly relinquished my role as cook when all men went "up top" to eat. What a joy to sit down and have a bologna sandwich!

We enjoyed entertaining visiting dignitaries from Great Britain, New Zealand and Australia. I recall Commander Ridge of England asking me, very politely, when I served blueberry pie, if it was sweetened. These were years when rationing was very rigid in his homeland.

I soon learned the Navy lingo: jetty for dock, galley for kitchen, mess hall was the dining room. It became almost an every day occurrence to rub shoulders with the "Big Brass" from somewhere.

I also discovered there were restrictions being the only woman at Camp. I never rode on the ships nor used the fine bathing beach while Camp was in. I went "up top" only on invitation.

For a few years summer meant moving completely out of the Winter House. Navy officers occupied it during the period when Camp was in. Like Gypsies we packed up cookstove, beds, and all our belongings. Down the hill we straggled.

The first year we retreated to the houseboat anchored alongside a rocky shoreline, out of sight yet still part of the island. There was a slant to the houseboat with the shore side being caught on a rocky ledge. We walked up hill into the house and down hill leaving the house.

The stove had bricks under the legs on the low side to make it level. There was a lace table cloth on the slanted table. Bonnie, by then a climber, crawled up on a chair, onto the table, wrapped the table cloth around herself and promptly fell off.

To go ashore we walked on a plank placed from the deck to the shore. Gary, the two and a half year old, with a stick of fire wood under each arm, stepped off the plank and went straight to bottom, feet first. For a few seconds he stood on bottom with four feet of water over his head. Finally, letting go of the wood, he bobbed to the surface sputtering and howling.

Mother Myers was aghast over the conditions her only daughter was living in. She and my dad had taken time to come by boat from Moon River to see us.

"Oh my!" she exclaimed, "I think you should come back and spend the summer with us."

I declined. I was satisfied in my make-shift quarters. Frank had been away for two and a half years in other parts of Canada and overseas with the Ordinance Corps. It was nice to be a family again.

The next year we were allowed to stay on the south east point, close to the Camp. From the Big Ark, one of the older cottages, we could watch the activities and move freely from the Rock Cottage dock in our boat.

Several years later Mr. Gordon C. Leitch decided to build us a permanent home, a house I designed. It was open concept in style, with large corner windows to bring the full beauty of the Bay into my home.

The first Sea Cadets arrived on the *M. V. Midland City*. We watched the young men, ages from twelve to eighteen, disembark with a duffel bag slung over a shoulder. Their round hats were set at just the right angle. Dressed in Navy blue, they marched off the long jetty.

Early in the morning I watched them take to the water at the sand beach. Cold or warm, sun, rain or fog, they were in the water by seven a.m. under the watchful eye of George West the swimming instructor. Their bodies, white on arrival, turned golden as the days passed.

The voice of Big Bob Pierce, former Australian sculler but a Canadian resident of many years, bellowing "hup, one-two-three" was easily heard as he put the cadets through their paces on the parade square.

My children were entranced by the whole procedure. They watched George West walking the length of the main jetty on his hands. His bronze body glistened in the sun, impressing Glen and Gary. They tried so hard to imitate him but small arms would give out and they flopped down on the grass to watch their hero.

It was fascinating to watch the cadets, two to a sailing dinghy, with their Mae West life preservers on, learning to maneuver the little craft in a frisky wind. There were many tip-overs and dunkings in the water before they became experts. A patrol boat was always close by to pull them out of Georgian Bay and tow the dinghy back to the big boathouse.

They had to learn to row the cutters and large whalers in unison and to march over the uneven rocks. The cadets from England excelled in precision marching over the pink granite of the Canadian Shield.

Private owners loaned their large boats to the "Service". It was difficult to obtain fuel of any kind during those war years. The harbour crafts, however, were the work boats, running into Midland each day for food supplies. But it was the *Chemonge*, the white sailing schooner, I enjoyed watching coming by John's Island under full sail with Lieutenant Smith in command. With cadets positioned on the tall rigging, he brought the white ship gracefully into the harbour.

At sunset the sound of the bugle echoed across the island. As the flag was slowly lowered from the masthead in front of the Administration building cadets stood at attention. The flag was then folded carefully without touching the ground.

There were days when I didn't see much of Frank. He was out the door at seven thirty and "up top" to the Administration building to speak with the commanding officer. At any time he could be either in Midland, Honey Harbour or the Queen Elizabeth Camp on Beausoleil.

Frank trained the Able Seamen to handle the harbour craft. He taught them the channel from the Camp to Midland that they had to take to pick up fresh supplies from the W. E. Preston store, just a short walk from the wharf. Prestons had served the town and the ships of the Great Lakes for years.

Milk was brought to Minnicog by the eight gallon can supplied by a local dairy. Huge quantities of meat and vegetables were needed to feed the four to five hundred persons aboard the island.

Sometimes, in the small hours of the morning, Frank would be called in to rush a sick cadet to Midland. There was always a doctor at Camp when cadets were in and, accompanied by the doctor and a padre, the young lad would be rushed twelve miles by boat through the dark night. I always sat up and waited until Frank returned and could tell me all was well.

I will never forget one such night. The island was quiet except for the fire watch. Occasionally, I saw their flashlights as they walked from building to building. I was reading and all was quiet in the house. Then the silence was broken by a tap-tap on the outside wall. I sat bolt upright, goose pimples popping out on my arms. The tap-tapping went all along the verandah. I hugged the book tightly trying to squeeze comfort from my only companion.

Later, I heard the hum of the boat, *Minnicog*. My courage rose a fraction and I hurried to the back kitchen to make a pot of coffee. When I struck a match to light the stove there was a terrific crash outside the door. I dropped the match in the stove, my hair stood on end and I thought my time had come. Slowly, I opened the door and looked outside to see a big, fat, frightened raccoon as he rushed away from the clattering garbage can lid.

One of the more memorable times was the day Lord Alexander of Tunis, the Governor General of Canada, came to visit Princess Alice Camp. Everything was ship-shape. I doubt if there was a blade of grass out of place on the parade square. Cadets were in white middies and bell-bottom trousers. Each round hat was the right number of inches above eyebrows. Commander Pearce, commander of the Camp, was in crisp summer whites.

Those of us who were to meet the Governor General, the nursing sister, dietician, myself and the officers, were mustered to the verandah. There was a delay in the party's arrival which included Midland's Mayor Charlie Stevenson and his wife. Tension mounted. The C.O. paced the deck, telescope in hand. The sun was setting low when word came: Frank had sighted the boat. We stood up, craned our necks and there, not far off, the *M.V. Georgian.*

The scene that greeted the Governor General was a crimson sunset over the island chain. He remarked later it was something he would never forget.

The sun had slipped down behind the trees. The western sky was a blaze of glory. When the boat carrying Lord Alexander approached the jetty, the cadets in cutters and whalers lifted their oars in salute against the breathtaking setting of Georgian Bay.

JETTY, "PRINCESS ALICE" NAVY LEAGUE SEA CADET CAMP, GEORGIAN BAY, ONTARIO

12 *(picture courtesy Bev Keefe)*

PREPARING FOR DINGHY RACE,
"PRINCESS ALICE" NAVY LEAGUE SEA CADET CAMP, GEORGIAN BAY, ONTARIO

13 *(picture courtesy Jack Lamoureux)*

14 The Sea Cadet band on the parade square *(picture by Jack Lamoureux)*

15 Sea Cadets marching up the hill *(picture by Jack Lamoureux)*

16 Rock Cottage

17 Main jetty with M.J. O'Rourke (Frank's brother) foreground & Narfield Dusome

18 Learning to sail on Minnicog Bay *(picture by Jack Lamoureux)*

19 Frank Rourke

20 Sea Cadets with Buzz

11

Cliff and Mary Paradis

Brébeuf Days

Cliff Paradis was born in Port Severn, Ontario. He spent his youth in and around Midland. Later he worked on the shore as a guide and lumberman.

It was on August 1, 1931, that he took over the position of lightkeeper at Brébeuf Ranges. The government ship the *St. Heliers*, which went into service that year, took him out to the station. The skipper of the ship was Captain Smith of Midland.

Brébeuf lighthouse stands a half mile off the shore of Beausoleil Island. It consists of the light tower, with dwelling attached and behind this is the tail light, a tall steel tower, situated on the shore of Beausoleil Island. These range lights are used to guide ships in from the outer bay to the ports of Midland, Port McNicoll and Penetanguishene.

Cliff's wife Mary was in hospital in Midland at the time and did not join her husband at the light until several weeks later.

The following year the Paradis' only child, a daughter, Jo-Ann was born.

When Cliff began his career as a lightkeeper lake freighters were all steam driven. There were no radio communications, the wireless caused so much static on the battery radio they couldn't understand what was being transmitted. Radar was unknown. During foggy weather the ship's whistles sounded over the bay as the ships groped their way through the fog.

Timber was the prime industry on the shore. During the summer months great rafts of logs were towed down to the mills in Penetanguishene by such tugs as the *Geraldine* and the *Francis M,* owned by Captain Bill Martin of Penetang.

There was no radio-phone communications at the lightstation either. The steamer *J.B. Hanna* went off course coming out of Midland harbour one stormy night. There was no way of warning the captain of the danger of the Osprey Bank lying northwest of the lighthouse and the ship ran up on the shoals.

Heavy gales prevented Cliff from reaching the distressed ship that night. The following morning the seas went down enough to let him go out in a rowboat and pull alongside.

The captain shouted to him to get in touch with the ship's company in Toronto and tell them of their plight.

Cliff walked across Beausoleil Island to the National Park headquarters. From there he was taken by boat to Honey Harbour. There were no telephones in the area so he hired a car which took him over the bumpy, rutted road to Midland where he telephoned Toronto.

The *J.B. Hanna* was pulled from the Osprey Bank the next morning and towed to Midland by a tug from the Burke Towing and Salvage Company.

"There has been a great fluctuation in the water level during the years," Cliff recalled. "Some years it would drop so low the island would be a few feet bigger all around. Other times it would be so high it would be over the dock. One year it came up so high during a nor'west gale the ice house and the rowboat were swept away."

The *Midland City*, The *City of Dover* and the *Water Bus*, boats out of Midland, were all familiar sights on the channel.

Getting on and off the light station at the opening and closing of the navigation season was usually an adventure.

"One year," Cliff said, "the government ship put us off at National Park headquarters. Peter Tonch took us and all our supplies across Beausoleil with a team of horses. We stayed in a small cabin at the tail light for two weeks until the ice cleared and we could move to the light."

"We played tag with the mice for the two weeks," Mary added with a hearty laugh.

Ice conditions often prevented the ship from getting into the light station in the spring. One year they were aboard ship for a week, going out as far as Griffith Island near Owen Sound, then back to Midland. Eventually they were put off at Minnicog Island. As a result, Cliff was the first lightkeeper to tend a light by scoot. He traveled back and forth with Frank until the ice cleared from the bay.

The following spring Cliff and Mary flew in, landing on a small strip of water near Minnicog. Once again Cliff tended light via scoot until the channel cleared.

Getting off the light station was just as adventurous.

"That first fall," Cliff recalled, "we ran a little low on food due to a lot of unexpected visitors. On the 17th of December we saw the government ship coming in the gap and we got all ready to go. It went right on by into Midland."

"My heart went to my boots," said Mary. "But they came back for us the next day."

"Another year we skated on two nights frost out to Gin Rock, pulling the baby on the sleigh, to get aboard the ship, and other years we have waded in snow across Beausoleil pulling our luggage on a toboggan.

The biggest adventure of all though, happened when they were caught out in one of Georgian 's swift, fierce summer storms. Gale force winds accompanied by thunder and lightning tossed their small boat about like a cork. Mary and her little dog were tossed out of the boat into the churning water at the beacon near Gendron's Channel. She managed to crawl ashore with the little dog under her arm. Later, Frank was able to rescue them.

During the same storm, a small boat owner sought shelter at the lighthouse. On leaving, he left a note to say he had been there and in his excitement he drove the ice-pick right through the kitchen table to hold the note in place.

Mary and Cliff became familiar figures on the shore. There was always a warm welcome and a bubbling coffee pot to welcome the stray, wet boaters when they drew into the shelter of Brébeuf.

Cliff believed that there was no better place to be than up the shore and both he and Mary made it a very much better place to be.

21 Cliff and Mary Paradis

22 Cliff Paradis, Frank Rourke and Buzz at Minnicog

12

School Days
Up The Shore

Moving to Minnicog meant moving to an area without any schools. Families living on the shore were scattered amongst the islands and mainland. Some children were struggling with correspondence courses from the Department of Education in Toronto. Others were growing up with no education.

When Glen, our oldest child, had passed age six and Gail was approaching school age, I decided I had to do something about the situation. Schooling had to come to the children of the area. Since we travelled by water it would have to be a seasonal school.

I recalled the school I attended when growing up in Moon River. Residents of the area were widely scattered then as well and hazardous ice conditions in the fall and spring made it impossible for the children to attend school ten months of the year.

Most of the pioneers of Moon River were educated people but they had raised a generation of children who never saw the inside of a school house. Some taught their children to read and write, others did not[10] .

Julius Arnold was the "father" of the first six month school. He had followed his cousin, Bill Myers, to Moon

---

10. Sometime between 1900 and 1909 a petition for a school in Moon River was sent to George Grant, Inspector of Public Schools at Orillia. The petition was signed by J. Leroux, Peter Gregoire, Mrs. Martin, F. Gregoire, George Elliot, James Crawford, Harry and Thomas Crawford, Dennis Sweet, William Longlade, C.W. Willett and Peter Cascanette. A meeting was called but only two people showed up.

River from their home town in southern Ontario. He was younger than many of his fellow pioneers and was raising a large family. He sent the first of his family to school in Parry Sound, all the while dreaming of a school in Moon River. He approached the Department of Education with his proposal.

The area known as Moon River was in two different districts. The Myers and Arnolds, who were the driving force behind the school, lived in Muskoka. But the larger population made up of the Gropps, Dions, Cascanettes, Longlades, Hudgins and Sweets lived in the district of Parry Sound.

It took many months and much negotiation to convince the districts that a six month school was possible. The difficult task of getting agreements between Freeman and Conger townships had to be done. Julius Arnold wanted the school on the Muskoka side of the boundary line but the Department of Education decided it would be in Conger.

The pioneer home of the Cascanette family, a large, one story building on an acre of land on the north side of the river was purchased from Judge Pollack, a summer resident from Kansas City, Kansas. Renovations were done and it became a one room school house.

Meanwhile, a three person school board was elected as well as a secretary treasurer. An advertisement was run in a Toronto paper for a teacher. Tenders were posted for a school boat for transporting of pupils to and from school. Both positions were filled and S.S. No. 2 Conger school opened its doors in 1921.

It was the era of the steam tug or the "one lunger" gasoline engine. Bob Arnold was one of the first school boat men. He thrilled the youngsters by having them join hands then have one of them touch the spark plug of the engine. The kid at the end of the line got the hardest jolt.

Herb Hudgins was another boat operator. He was a short, little man with a boat shaped like a box and top heavy. When it would get into a heavy sea he would shout, "Climb for the high side!" The children scrambled quickly, afraid it would tip over and dump them in the river.

Charlie Sweet, who had merry blue eyes and a hearty laugh, was the school boat man for most of my school years. He had a good boat, was always prompt and made the trip down and up the river safe and pleasant.

It was necessary to employ a second boat after a time. One covered the route up river, the other to Gropps and Iron City and, much later, even out to Sans Souci area until a school was built at Sugar Bay on the westerly tip of Moon Island.

"Bun" Gregoire was the man who picked up the children of the islands every school morning, taking them in through the Captain Allen Straits to S.S. #2 Conger. At four o'clock he was back at the school dock helping the life-belted youngsters into his covered boat for the trip home.

Teachers came from many places in Ontario. Several had university degrees but most were graduates of Normal School. Some went on from teaching in our one room shore school to teach in universities. Another became a public school inspector.

The school year began as soon as the river and Bay were mostly ice free. Time was needed to get the boats running and to get to Parry Sound to pick up the teacher, usually around May first.

When Allie and I saw the school boat coming we grabbed our books and lunch boxes. Down to the dock we went to wait until the school boat pulled alongside. We climbed aboard and headed down river to the brown school house.

We sized up the new teacher out of the corner of our eyes. Usually it was a different teacher each year. Some innocent soul whose destiny took them thirty miles over water from the nearest town, Parry Sound. They seemed to adjust to the isolation. I cannot recall any of them going to town during the six months. A local girl, Julia Arnold, taught one year. Another year the young teacher married Bob Arnold sometime after the school term was finished.

The school season went right through the hot months of July and August. Our school yard was as barren as the Sahara Desert. How we envied the cattle from Sweet's farm lounging beneath the spreading maple and oak trees on the other side of the fence.

Picture following page:

S.S. Number 2, Conger School, Moon River, 1930

Left to Right:Back Row: Marie Grisdale, Margaret Bissonette, Winnie Hudgins, Laval Martin, Peter Grisdale, 'Buddy' Martin, Wilfred Cascanette, Leo Martin
Middle Row: Peter Cascanette, Beverley Bissonette, Isaac Hudgins, Juanita Myers (Rourke), Jessie Hudgins, Jane Hudgins Front Row: Nelson Cascanette, Norma Hudgins, Marshall Grisdale
(These three Hudgins were killed by lightning one night as they slept)

31 Class of 1930

(picture courtesy Pete Grisdale)

School continued through the cool, windy months of fall and we wrote our final exams in October.

The most nerve wracking time during the year was the visit of the school inspector. At the sound of his foot steps on the porch, every pupil was gripped with terror. We were afraid we wouldn't know the answers to the questions he asked, having to face embarrassment in the classroom or irate parents at home if we didn't meet their expectations. We were always on our best behaviour and studied really hard before he came.

After passing grade eight, the entrance examinations, as they were called then, to high school had to be written in Parry Sound. For three days we had to board in town, had to make our way to a strange school which appeared huge and frightening to a shore kid. To write these Departmental exams we were put in with unfamiliar students under the watchful eye of an unfamiliar teacher. Frightening as it was, every pupil from the six month school who wrote over the years managed to pass into high school.

Tragedy struck our little group on a hot summer night, a night of lightning and thunder rolling across the river.

There were twenty of us in class that year. It was a year when the favourite saying was: "I'll see you in the funny papers." I've forgotten the origin but never the words.

It was Friday afternoon, a hot, humid sort of day. We were all clambering aboard the boats, anxious to get home to go swimming.

The five Hudgins children got in the boat heading towards Woods Bay while I got in the school boat going up river.

"See you in the funny papers." Isaac, the twelve year old, hollered as we pulled away from the dock.

Isaac and his young sisters, Winnie and Norma were killed by lightening that week-end.

Our little group was stunned. We understood the power of nature because we lived closely to it but we couldn't understand why it took away our friends.

A six month school was built at Point Au Baril after the Moon River school was opened. When a road reached the settlement the island school closed and a regular school was opened on the mainland.

Now I was in need of a school for my own children. I talked to the other people of the shore and they were very interested. I decided to take action towards getting a school. I wrote the Department of Education in Toronto and through their co-operation and with the help of the public school inspector from Orillia, the school district No. 1 Gibson and Baxter emerged.

This did not happen easily. Much time and effort went into it! A petition was made up. Frank and I went by boat from the home of one parent to the next, from Franceville in the Freddy Channel to Cognashene where the Robitaille and King families lived. They all signed the petition. We counted the school age children and had enough to open a school.

A school board was formed. I was secretary, Jack Birks, treasurer. An assessment roll was also made up.

The following spring the first classroom was opened in Emery O'Rourke's living room. Peggy, my sister-in-law, co-operated with the unusual situation in her home. We scrounged black boards and desks from the island school in Honey Harbour which had been closed for some time.

Mrs. Leola McCutcheon of Lions Head, whose husband was a lake Captain, was our first teacher at S.S. #1 Gibson and Baxter. Having taught in Moon River, she was experienced with the shore school system.

Emery O'Rourke operated the first school boat. Later, Wilf France took over making the run morning and night from Franceville to Minnicog and on to Cognashene.

Later in the season the classroom was moved from the O'Rourke house to a houseboat. The same houseboat the horse and I travelled to Minnicog in. Emery bought the houseboat and pulled it up on shore.

I remember, vividly, putting worn carpets on the floor and stuffing rags around the windows to cut down the draft in late fall.

The first pupils ranged in age from six years to a girl of fifteen who had never been to school. She covered two grades in the one short season.

It was a rough start in our quest for an education for the children. It was not over by any means. We were met with much opposition from the summer residents of Gibson township. They wondered about this nonsense of a school for resident children. Why should they have to pay school taxes when they already paid enough on their city property?

"And," said one old-time cottager, "educate them and they'll want more wages."

A meeting was called in mid summer for the school board. The secretary and the school inspector were to meet a delegation of summer residents headed by Judge McGibbon of Lindsay. I heard rumors of the dire things that would happen to me at that meeting.

"The Judge will tear you apart." I was warned.

With some apprehension and a great deal of determination I attended the meeting held at the Franceville Hotel on the Freddy Channel.

I was ready for a confrontation that never materialized. The meeting was very congenial. Judge McGibbon was understanding and co-operative.

"You deserve a school," he said, shaking our hands.

When the meeting was over, Mr. Gibson, the school inspector and I heaved a sigh of relief. Now we could seek a permanent school building.

A parcel of land was acquired on the south eastern shore of Cognashene Lake. Celest Robitaille had a building available. He moved it during the winter, on the ice, to the school property. Renovations were made and when the school year began in May, the children of the shore had a school of their own.

The George Bush family moved to Muskoka Mills and the school boat route expanded to include them. Phil Robitaille of Cognashene took over the run and, with a cheerful grin, he assumed the responsibility of the kids to and from the hard earned school.

Mrs. McCutcheon returned to the shore and taught for several years in the one room school house.

Later, a similar school system was opened in Go Home Bay.

From its humble beginning, S.S. # 1 Gibson and Baxter school accomplished what we worked so hard for, education for our children.

Changes have come over the years. Modern winter transportation and roads make it possible for shore children to have equal opportunity with all young Canadians. However, the six month school served us well when the horse was the only means of winter transportation up the shore of eastern Georgian Bay and going to school meant travelling by boat.

I am certain that Julius Arnold, the person responsible for this special school system, would have said in his quiet spoken way, "Well done."

61 The one room school house class of 1949 Cognashene

The Rourke, O'Rourke, France, Robitaille, King, and Bush, families

13

Supply Boats

The first tourists to find the shore were mainly wealthy Americans. They moved in with much grandeur around the first part of July and stayed until the later part of August, bringing with them their cooks, housemaids and butlers. Caretakers and guides were hired from among the men on the shore.

Judge Pollock of Kansas City and Isaac Scott, a steel magnate from Wheeling West Virginia, paddled down the Moon River and pitched tents on their chosen islands. Later, they built cottages. Several generations of Scotts and Pollocks have vacationed in Moon River.

An Oklahoma oil baron, a justice of the Supreme Court of the U.S.A., all found their way to the shore. The Breithaupts from Kitchener, Ontario, joined them.

The Iron City Fishing Club gave up their original site at Go Home Bay and set up their tent city near Captain Allen Straits. A small store at Sans Souci served as a post office and grocery store. It was built alongside the Sans Souci Hotel which was operated by the Grisé brothers who eventually opened the Royal and Delawana hotels in Honey Harbour. The floor of the beverage room in the Royal Hotel was originally the floor of the Sans Souci hotel.

The Mandelbaums built their lodge on Somerset Island. The Yankanuck Club, with its large white club house, was established by a group of Americans. B. H. Prack was nearby. Mr. Clark, Lieutenant Governor of Ontario and the Ludwigs all settled in the Sans Souci area and Wah Wah Taysee was established by the Nesbitts and Beattys.

27 The *City Queen*

Sir Wm. Mulock, Post Master General of Canada was one of the original members of the Tadanac Club. The faculty of the University of Toronto set up an establishment at Go Home Bay. Whalens was a post office and landing place for the Muskoka Mills and Minnicognashene was the finest summer resort on the shore.

Supply boats were a very important part of summer life on the shore for many, many years. To these establishments, the hotels, clubs and others, the supply boats were the floating grocery store. The *Maud Davidson*, a steam boat for the Playfair and Preston Company out of Midland, was the first supply boat. The large ships landed at the bigger establishments such as Minnicog, Whalens, Go Home Bay, Somerset, Yankanuck and Sans Souci. Tourists converged on the docks by rowboat and smaller motor boats to pick up their weekly supplies. The *City Queen*, sixty to eighty feet long, followed the *Maud Davidson* in the service to summer residents until it burned at Manitou. Following that, smaller boats gave cottage to cottage service to about ninety per cent of the summer population. The Midland supply boats ranged as far north as the Sans Souci area, and the *John P.* out of Parry Sound was the last supply boat to service that area closing down in the 1950's.

Each supply boat was set up with counters and shelves, much like a regular store. They carried almost anything you might need such as flour, sugar, spices, cereal, canned goods, as well as meats, eggs, fruits and vegetables.

The boats were fueled over the course of the years by wood, coal, gasoline and diesel.

The *Shuffle Along*, a gasoline supply boat from Parry Sound, was a familiar sight for many years on the shore. Not only did it deliver gas and oil to the islands, but in the fall it would deliver tons of oats and hay to the residents to feed their horses and cattle over the winter. The *Shuffle Along* can be seen alongside Highway 69 about fourteen miles south of Parry Sound, a sentimental monument to a bygone era on the shore.

The tug *Geraldine*, out of Penetang, provided the same service in the fall as the *Shuffle Along*. Tons of hay, oats and other supplies were delivered from Penetang to Johnny Martin at Wah Wah Taysee.

2 Preston's Supply Boat (*picture by Bev Keefe*)

60 The *Geraldine*

14

Muskoka Mills
The Forgotten Village

To the thousands of tourist plying the waters up the shore, the mouth of the Musquash River is a good spot to bass fish, have a picnic, frolic in the water of the busy little rapids and drink in the tranquility of the scene. Most do not realize they are looking at the site of what was once the largest settlement on the shore between Midland and Parry Sound.

Muskoka Mills came into being in the mid 1850's and had, during its peak, a population of two hundred or more people.

It was thirteen miles across water from Penetanguishene. It had a post office, school, Union Church, stores and three saw-mills, saw mills which produced saw-dust as well as lumber.

We were in need of saw-dust for the huge ice-house at Princess Alice Camp and Wilf France of Franceville on the Freddy Channel told Frank there was a plentiful supply at Saw Dust Bay. One pretty day we headed for the Musquash to inquire from the caretaker of the estate, Rod Patenaude, about getting some of the saw-dust .

The sun sparkled on the water and the islands seemed to be floating, an illusion that occurs in the fall of the year.

I had not met any of the year 'round residents of the shore so I eagerly accepted Frank's offer to go along for the ride in the *Minnicog*.

On the way to Rod Patenaude's we passed Penetang Rock, then Lambert Island, which was, at that time, the summer residence of the famous Orville Wright. In 1916 Orville Wright, his sister and father, Bishop Wright, rented the Williams family cottage, fell in love with the Bay, bought Lambert Island and spent summers there until his death. His boat, the *Kitty Hawk*, was purchased by Wilf France and remains in the family to this day.

The Wright cottage stood on the summit of the island with nothing to obstruct the view of Georgian Bay as far as the eye could see.

We ran by Ship Island, so called because vessels kept close to avoid the Otonabee shoal. I sat in the seat at the stern of the boat wondering, as we passed Sugar Island, how it had been named.

The *Minnicog* was a comfortable boat with high sides and plenty of floor room. It was safe for the children and could carry a good load. It was built by the Ulrichson Brothers of Penetanguishene for C.W. Beatty, a Toronto lawyer with a summer estate at Wah Wah Taysee. The hull was painted grey but the cabin was all mahogany and glass. The interior was lined with mahogany as well. A *Buchanan* motor hummed inside the varnished engine box in the centre of the boat.

The *Minnicog*, easy to handle, gentle in the heavy seas, was first known by the name *Mindamoya* and driven by Johnny Martin, Frank's brother-in-law who was caretaker for the Beatty estate. It served us well for ten years.

Rod Patenaude was at the dock to take the lines of our boat. He was a wiry man with short cropped grey hair, twinkling brown eyes and a puckish smile. He escorted us up to the house, the only one remaining of the mill town buildings. He captivated the children by giving them each a "pounder" apple from the tree growing alongside the pathway. One apple was almost large enough to make a pie.

Before taking the job as caretaker of the McCarthy estate, Rod had operated the shunter at Beck Mills in Penetanguishene. The shunter was a small locomotive that moved the railway cars around in the yard to be loaded with lumber. The shunter Rod operated has been located on the grounds of the Penetanguishene Museum for many years, not far from the town docks.

Over several cups of tea I learned something of the village of Muskoka Mills. I was interested in the dock we had landed at. It was almost water level, broken down and over grown with Tagalders and weeds.

"Oh, the dock," Rod explained, "it is the remainder of the slab docks built of green slabs from the mills." This slab dock continued for two and a half miles along the shore and was used as one long loading platform. Lumber was piled on the docks, then transferred to barges which carried it across the Bay and Lake Huron.

Rod drew our attention to a bare seventy foot high point south of the mill site. All refuse from the mills was burned there creating a huge amount of smoke which could be seen for miles around.

"It was quite a sight," said Rod, "when the three mills were going full blast."

I learned more about the history of the village as I became more acquainted with the area.

It was early 1875, so I was told, when a Mr. Campbell obtained the business from T.C. Hughson and Company. He also obtained two hundred and seventy-four square miles of timber limits. Timber limits were lands obtained from the Crown with a licence issued to the lumbering company to remove timber from a designated area.

32 Rod Patenaude beside shunter (*picture courtesy Joe Patenaude*)

There was great activity during the season when tens of thousands of logs were driven down the Musquash, spilling into the Bay where they were contained by booms. River drivers sorted the logs in "pointers", narrow punt-like craft, pointed at both bow and stern.

Mill hands fed the logs into the teeth of the big gang saws. The whine of the saws were heard twelve hours every day. The smell of freshly cut lumber hung in the air. Slabs cut from logs fed the boiler to keep the steam up to run the saws.

The lumber, loaded on hand carts, was hauled by hand to the yards. Pine boards were piled to a height of thirty feet on the slab docks along the shoreline.

I tried to visualize what it must have been like to watch the barges pulling alongside. Many were sailing schooners towed in through the narrow channel by tugs, channels like the Freddy where it was impossible for big ships to maneuver under sail. When loaded, the schooners were towed back out to open water.

Lumber piled at Muskoka Landing (now Whalen's Island) was used to top off a load on some of the larger vessels drawing too much water for passage through the inside channel.

One tug involved in towing schooners was the *Sweet Mary* owned by Captain Bill Martin of Penetanguishene. The Martins were also involved in log towing, log picking and salvaging bark.

The Muskoka Mills was the hub of much activity. There was daily mail service by steam tug from Penetanguishene. Groceries and supplies came in for the company store by boat and there were constant comings and goings of people from the mainland. There were Saturday night square dances with a fiddler or two to provide music and someone to call the sing-song - "grab your partner and whirl around the floor." On Sundays there was always a church service in the mornings and the workers spent the afternoons relaxing and visiting amongst each other.

The importance of the village was emphasized in the 1894 edition of *The Georgian Bay and North Channel Pilot* issued by the Department of Marine and Fisheries, Ottawa. The little book, which I inherited from my grandfather Myers, gave detailed sailing directions to the Muskoka Mills.

Life at the mill town was relatively quiet in the winter. Most of the men were out in the bush cutting the white pine to feed the mills the next summer.

Winter was the time to harvest the trees. The lakes and rivers were frozen and there was plenty of snow in the bush for the sleigh to haul the logs.

In the village, life carried on, with skating for the children when the ice was safe, quilting bees and sometimes visitors from town arriving by horse and cutter.

In 1895 the Muskoka Mills closed down. The hills of Muskoka had been stripped of pine. There was no more for the mills. Machinery was dismantled and sold to a company further north. People, some born in the village, moved away. The board walks, school, church and houses disappeared. Nature took over and covered much of the site.

What remains are small remnants of a lumbering village that prospered on the shore for almost half a century. Bits of broken crockery are scattered about the green moss, in the grey sawdust of Saw Dust Bay and can be seen among the slabs from the mill on the river bottom. Iron rings in the rocks at the river's bend, which held the booms across its mouth, are still there.

One day, later in the summer when Frank had some time off, we went to the Musquash on a warm afternoon. We packed a picnic and invited a few of the Navy League personnel to join us.

The children and I went up river to swim while Frank and friends stayed to fish. When it came time to eat, a circle of stones formed a make-shift fireplace. Frank was chef and an expert at cooking freshly caught fish to a golden perfection.

We stopped dockside on our way home to say hello to Rod and his daughter Florence, who had come to stay with him. Rod was leaving Muskoka Mills after these many years and George Bush was taking over the caretaking of the McCarthy estate. Like his uncle Archie Brock, George had been caretaker at the Tadnac Club near Wah Wah Taysee.

We became friends with George and his family and have shared in each others joys and sorrows over the years.

34 George Bush (*picture by Bev Keefe*)

15

Winter Babies

The arrival of the stork at freeze-up time on the shore was a complicated business. It meant leaving home before the freeze-up set in and not returning until well after the new year when the ice was thick on the Bay. It meant a forlorn Christmas day in strange surroundings.

We were living on Somerset Island at Sans Souci when Gail was born in 1939. Winter travel was still by horse and sleigh. The Scoot had not been introduced to the shore, aircraft travel was undreamed of and the snowmobile was in the distant future.

So, it was off to Parry Sound by boat on a cold November day and a six week sojourn with cousins at Nobel where everything was wild with war contract activity. On December twenty-nine our dark haired daughter was born in Parry Sound General Hospital; born in a public ward with curtains drawn around the bed.

Two weeks later we took her home. On a brisk, cold day with the temperature standing at sixteen degrees below zero farenheit, we tucked her in a pasteboard carton box with a hot water bottle beside her. We drove by car to Rosseau where Frank had stabled the horse. My grandmother, Elizabeth Palmer Myers, who had given birth to her baby in a tent many years before, had spent the freeze-up in Orillia and was travelling with us; grandmother and her huge trunk which Frank cursed every step of the way.

Baby, grandmother, myself and the trunk were loaded in the sleigh. The people at Rosseau thought we were out of our minds venturing out with such a small baby on such a wintery day. Now that I think of it, so do I.

The horse we owned was good for nothing but crow bait. It was so ancient its teeth were ready to fall out. The result was he could not chew his hay. Frank had to buy crushed oats so the horse could get some nourishment. Frank and my brother Allie pushed the sleigh over the portages. Grandmother and I walked behind. We made our way down Crane Lake facing a fierce wind all the way. There was slush on Pine Lake which meant walking most of the way. Finally, we emerged at Blackstone Harbour with only a mile or so to go to Mother Myers house.

There was a steep hill to climb at Martin's Portage. Sea Biscuit, the horse, took one look at it, lay down between the shafts and refused to move. So the men unhitched him and decided to pull the sleigh up the hill themselves. No sooner was Sea Biscuit unhitched than he leaped to his feet and bolted up the hill like a two year old. My brother bolted after him and caught him half way across the portage.

We finally made it! After the men dragged the sleigh up the hill they hitched the reluctant horse to it and he trudged slowly across Woods Bay. Mother and Father Myers were on the back step with Glen, waiting for us. Frank hurriedly handed the carton containing Gail to Mother Myers. When a happy and tearful "Nanna" opened the box she found her granddaughter snug and warm, fast asleep. We never forgot that trip and Frank never forgot that trunk of grandmother's .

About two years after we arrived at Minnicog, the stork once again hovered around at freeze-up. Off I went with three youngsters, Gail, Gary and Bonnie, to stay with a friend in Midland leaving Glen, the oldest, with Frank at Minnicog. It was a long four months before I returned, leaving in November and returning to my beloved island in mid-February. How grown up Glen seemed and how I had missed him!

Garnet Edward was born at five past twelve New Years morning, 1945. He was Midland's New Year's baby. We took our son home six weeks later on a warm, sunny February day by horse and sleigh - a swifter horse and no trunk to weigh down the back of the sleigh.

Two years later, in December, Gillard John was born. He was a month old before Frank knew he had another son. There were no radio 'phones to send messages by and Scoots and aircraft were yet to come to the shore.

With a sad heart, I had left Minnicog for Midland in late November, taking only Garnet with me. Frank was on his own to play Santa for Glen, Gail, Gary and Bonnie and to bake a birthday cake for Gail on December twenty-ninth. He did just fine even though there was a cow to milk twice a day in a barn a great distance from the house, a horse to water and feed and four little kids to take care of.

Freeze-up was late that year. The weather remained too warm to let the ice freeze solid enough for Frank to get off the island with the children. By mid January I was weary of waiting in Midland and anxious to be with my family. I talked to Narfield and Leonard Dusome at Highland Point. They worked for Frank in the winter and had a dog team.

I asked them to take a run to Minnicog. Without hesitation, they left for the island. Leonard returned with a message. Narfield would baby sit while Frank and Leonard met me at Saw Log Bay. The following day I was on my way.

25 Garnet and Gillard with their Mom, Juanita Rourke, at the Winter House

I took a taxi to Grozzel's farm on the outskirts of Northwest Basin. From there we went by horse and sleigh to Joe Grisdales at Saw Log Bay where Frank was waiting to see his new son. The big black team floundered chest deep in snowdrifts several times, making us fearful for the baby in the box.

The wind was strong from the nor'west. Blustering snow rose in swirls high above the ice, with only the tops of the trees of Minnicog visible to show us the way. Frank put the cardboard box holding his new son on the dog sleigh, placed Garnet behind the box and wrapped him in a blanket. I knelt on the space that was left.

The dogs were anxious to go, yelping and barking in their excitement. Frank and Leonard kept up a steady trot beside the team as they ran across the ice and snow. It was late afternoon when Gillard arrived at our island home at the end of a very long journey but, only the first of many he would make across Georgian Bay.

And so, in December of each year, I remember a young woman, babies in boxes and the journeys that brought them home.

The following is an excerpt quoted directly from a newspaper clipping I saved from a Toronto newspaper. It was the summer of 1948.

"A ceremony of local and widespread interest took place on Monday, August 18, on Minnicog Island in Georgian Bay, when the Chaplain of the Fleet, the Rev. E. G. B. Foote O.B.E. (R.C.N.)[11]*, assisted by the Rev. James Norquay, baptized Gillard John, Garnet Edward and Bonnie Gaye, the three youngest children of Mr. and Mrs. C. E. (Frank) Rourke, of Minnicog Island.*

The guests present included Lieutenant Commander E. B. Pearce, Naval Officer in charge, Lieutenant Commander Robert Pearce, Staff Officer, Lieutenant Commander H. G. R. Williams, Staff Officer of Queen Elizabeth Sea Cadet Camp, Beausoleil Island, Mr. J. Handley Smith, Navy League Camp Representative, Toronto, Mr. Harry R. Gillard, Dominion Secretary, Navy League of Canada and Mr. John Fulton Gillard of Oakville.

---

1. Rev. E.G.B. Foote O.B.E. (R.C.N.),VC was awarded the Victoria Cross in WW II

A dainty repast was later served to the guests in the Navy League Guest House which was delightfully decorated with flowers for the occasion.

A silver baptismal cup, suitably inscribed to commemorate the ceremony, was presented by John Gillard, godfather to Gillard John Rourke."

The Chaplain of the Fleet, the Rev. E. G. B. Foote, O.B.E., (RCN), VC, had flown from Halifax to Toronto, drove to Midland by car and was transported by boat to Minnicog for the ceremony. This military ceremony was a rare honour for a civilian family and one I have never forgotten.

24 A military honour for a civilian family

Left to right: John Gillard, H.R. Gillard,Dominion Sec. of Navy League,
                    Lt. Com. Bob Pearce, Rev. E.G.B. Foote, O.B.E. (RCN),VC,
                    Chaplain of the Fleet,
                    Lt. Com E.B. Pearce, Frank Rourke (holding Gillard John),
                    Lt. Com. H.G.R. Williams, J. HandleySmith
                    In Front: Juanita Rourke, Glen, Gary, Gail, Garnet and Bonnie

16

Berry Picking Up The Shore

When summer comes on full force the sun shines, rain pelts down and acres of blueberries appear as if by magic on bald rocks and along rocky hillsides.

The hills of Muskoka along the Moon River is one place where blueberries grow. Even the rocky islands, Minnicog, Brébeuf and some smaller islands, have their hidden patches. Long ago, before there were rows of cans on the store shelves, everyone was out on the hills with their pails picking blueberries. It is usually late July before the crop starts to ripen.

I have trotted more miles than I care to think of behind my parents picking blueberries. I hated it! The sun beating down on our heads, deer flies taking great chunks out of my bare legs, tripping over fallen logs, all the while I was just trying to fill up my little honey pail with blueberries.

It seemed to take a long time to cover the bottom of the pail. Each berry went thump when it hit the tin bottom.

"Pick them clean," said Father Myers. So I didn't dare let a green one or a leaf into the pail.

I had trouble enough filling the bottom half, but the top half crept up so slowly I was usually close to tears by the time the can was full and I was finished.

If I had not eaten so many the pail would have been filled sooner, but what child could resist the warm, sun ripened fruit.

Father Myers always carried a large milk pail. I don't know how many quarts it held, but it was big.

If the berrying was good he could fill it in an hour. He knew where all the best spots were and I could hear the dry sticks crack under his feet as he worked his way through the patch.

Mother Myers was pretty expert at picking and, being a thrifty Scots woman, she appreciated getting something free. My brother grudgingly filled his ten pound syrup can. I think he hated picking berries as much as I did.

Father Myers worked for the tourists and was absent every day of the week from seven in the morning until nine o'clock at night. Like all the men on the shore he got about $3.50 a day for operating the boats, going out fishing with the American tourists, cleaning the fish and fetching in the firewood.

He was also responsible for getting the blocks of ice out of the ice house, washing off the sawdust and cutting them to fit the ice-box in the kitchen. He painted the cottage, built wooden sidewalks, hob-nobbed with the millionaires and never missed a days work because the big money making season only lasted two months.

So, in berry season, Mother would lead my brother and me on a picking expedition through the week.

I liked the walk through the woods with the dry moss cracking underfoot.

One hot August day when the wind was light and everything was silent except for the hum of insects, Mother led us up the North Hill past Myers Lake along a foot path shaded by spruce and pine, up a juniper covered slope and into a huge patch of blueberries.

The sun beat down, the silence was almost deafening. Mother settled down on the far side, my brother higher up. I found the shade of a scraggy little oak tree.

The berries thumped in the pails, a chipmunk chattered from the top of a dry stump. From the other side of the hill came a strange sound.

I felt little stabs of apprehension on the back of my neck. Mother's straw hat came up out of the berry patch. She looked up at my brother standing on the hill above us.

We heard it again, a loud roar from the other side of the hill.

"A bear," my mother hollered. She was on her feet by then, the berry pail flew in one direction and she tore off down the hill.

My brother charged past me and was in the lead before I could gather my wits. I was seven years old and my legs were trembling.

Something in those huge, lovely woods was making a terrible noise and I was being abandoned. Before I could make up my mind to run, the lonesome sound of a train's whistle echoed over the hills.

Mother stopped still. "It's only a train at MacTier," she exclaimed and the sound of her laughter filled the woods. That was one thing about her, she could laugh when the rest of us quaked in our boots.

We went back to berry picking but we were all a little skittish so the pails were never filled that day. We giggled as we walked towards home. I think my brother, being twelve, felt a little foolish over the fact he had been spooked so easily.

When I think of it now, we had wild animals all around us in those days but we never had a moment's serious trouble with any of them.

Next to picking berries, I hated cleaning them.

Even though we were told to pick the berries clean, the odd leaf and branch sneaked in.

On the way home though, I thought about the delicious blueberry pie we would have for supper. The crust would be rich and flaky, sugar and a bit of flour mixed in with the berries for the filling and a bit of juice oozing out through the holes in the top crust while it cooked. These were not just plain holes to let out the steam because mother always made some fancy design on the top of all her pies.

It amuses me now when I don't bake a pie because the electric stove might heat up the kitchen. It was just as hot in those days and there was no insulation in the house to stave off the heat.

The stove was a wood burning, cast iron monster. My brother and I would gather tan-bark off the logs that had come down river in the spring. The bark was dry and made a quick, hot fire. The stove was lit early in the morning before the sun soared overhead.

Most of the berries picked during the summer were put down for the winter which was quite a job in those days.

The reservoir, a copper lined well on the end of the cook stove next to the oven, was filled with water. The stove was fired up and the water heated while mother sorted out the quart jars, checked the screw tops and fetched the new rubber rings she had bought in Parry Sound from the pantry shelf.

The jars, tops, and rubber rings were washed in a dish pan filled with warm water and soap. They were set in a pan of water on top of the stove to be sterilized while the berries, mixed with granulated sugar, slowly came to a boil, turning to a deep purple colour as they reached a rolling boil.

Wood had to be added to the fire box frequently to keep things boiling, making the kitchen seem like an oven as well. It did not take long to fill up the jars, to screw on the lids and stand them in a row on the kitchen table.

This was only one of many such sessions until a hundred quarts or more were stored away on the pantry shelves under the stairway.

They were mighty handy to have when winter lay over the land. If a neighbor from some distant part of the shore dropped in, dessert was no problem when there was plenty of home made bread and a jar of blueberries on the table.

17

Howling Winds

A wild, raging giant was loose over the Bay. A wind of tremendous proportions swooped off Lake Huron, buffeted the islands, twisted the trees and crashed the weaker ones to the ground. The west wind pushed the water up to its all time high level, swirling over the docks, bouncing the Fisher and the outboard, pushing the scow until it strained on its heavy ropes.

The giant roared in late in the afternoon. Inch by inch the water crept up until, by darkness, it had risen at least two feet. Huge waves rolled down the gap over and over until they crashed in a wild spray against the rocky shoreline, a spray that froze as soon as it hit the rocks or hung in icicles from the little bushes that cling to the crevices near the shore.

With Frank and the children away, I watched the boats with apprehension. I could see them bobbing up and down by the light shining from the front of the house. Time and again I dropped my knitting to glance out the window. Around eight o'clock I noticed the little green outboard was missing. I debated going down to the dock and then I took the flashlight and, with my jacket buttoned tightly, I opened the door. Dry leaves whirled in on the wings of the wind and skimmed across the kitchen floor as I hurried out. Our big Newfoundland dog, Buzz, followed me down the path. The wind had a bite to it and it pushed and tore at me as I struggled against it. I swept the length of the dock with the flashlight. The outboard and motor were gone in the night and the wild water discouraged me from going out to look for it. After checking the lines on the other boats and the scow

I raced up the path toward the warmth and safety of the house. A million screaming demons seemed to chase me and when I opened the door a dozen or more dry leaves flew into the house.

The wind and water conditions can change quickly. Just the morning before, when Frank and I headed the Fisher toward Brébeuf, the wind was in the east, rolling down at us over the hills of Beausoleil. It was a sharp, damp wind with flecks of snow in it that stung the eyes. Even with my red parka pulled tight and a grey blanket over my knees, the wind penetrated to my very bones as the boat scurried through the Bull's Eye at Gendron's Channel.

With the leaves gone from the trees and the rocks grey and washed looking, there is a lonely look to a lighthouse in the fall of the year. The island of Brébeuf, with its smooth flat rocks, seemed shrunken. The white lighthouse looked forlorn sitting amidst the vast waters of "Manitou." Easterly winds had pushed the water far to the west leaving the docks high on the shore. The log piers with stones protruding looked grotesque and ungainly. Peter and Jenny, the spaniels, stood well above us as we pulled into the dock.

I hurried up the rock strewn path to the warmth of the lighthouse kitchen. The next few hours were spent pleasantly with our friends the Paradis' discussing the weather, the absence of boats, reminiscing of other falls and freeze-ups.

The wind was at our back as we headed back to Minnicog. Later, Frank hauled lumber with the tractor to the other side of the island where the men were working. I followed back and forth for a while as the tractor and trailer waddled over the rocks and through the swampy spots. I took time to pick a bunch of bittersweet from a swamp at the southerly side of the island. The swamp, a fairly large one, is a mass of red end to end. As I picked my way through the swamp I thought of Christmas and hoped that mother partridge would leave a few of the berries for the big day.

As the afternoon waned the men hinted that a cup of coffee would hit the spot. I wandered back through the woods and down the side hill to the house, brewed a pot full of coffee, made some sandwiches and packed it all in a basket. The coffee pot tipped as I climbed the hill and my foot tingled as hot coffee hit my instep. Just as my arm seemed to be breaking off with the weight of the pot, brother-in-law Emery came to my rescue and helped me carry it over to the far side of the island.

The coffee steamed as I poured it into the cups that I set in a row on the deck of the scow. As we stood by the water's edge with the cups warming our cold hands, snow came drifting over Cedar Point. Slowly it crept across the gap until it whirled around us with fluffy, soft flakes falling into the steaming coffee.

The next morning the wind was still in the east. It was raw and filled with rain. The water was at its lowest ebb and the little bay in front of the house was dry for the first time in six years. Slime covered rocks and shoals stood out while the rain pelted down on them. At three-thirty the wind died. The Bay was a mirror and the trees stood still.

"The wind is going to change direction," said Frank.

At four p.m. the first breeze came whipping out of the west and the surface of the water darkened. Quickly the wind mounted in fury and for twenty-four hours it thrashed and battered the Bay in a maddened rage. The strength of it was frightening as it continued its rampage over our land.

By Friday the Bay had changed again. The wind had spent itself and had drifted to the north. A thin skim of ice covered the Bay and the ground underfoot was frozen hard. Mother Nature was warning the folks who live up the shore that freeze-up time is 'nigh, they'd better scurry off to town for their last minute shopping before Jack Frost takes over and hems them in for another winter.

18

Halloween at Minnicog

Oh how the witches, the ghosts and the goblins floated over the rocks of Minnicog on Halloween. A more frightening assortment never before invaded the quiet dignity of the Administration Building. There was a goblin, with the floppiest ears imaginable, whose stuffing kept dropping around its knees. There was a strange looking creature in a suit of long underwear and a monstrous stomach and a ghost whose sheet kept fluttering in the cold north wind.

"Oh, I stepped in a puddle!" complained one little goblin. "Watch out for the water pipe!" But the warning came too late. A witch fell head over heels knocking her hat askew.

Up the stone steps they went, past the guest house whose friendly lights are shut off for the season, on to the biggest building of all, the main house, where they were going to keep a rendezvous with the ghost of Colonel Cautley who, no doubt, was keeping a lonely vigil in the great Manor House.

"That must be Daddy," was one comment as the frightful figure in the long underwear marched ahead. "Gail would never be brave enough to go first."

Across the wide verandah they paraded. S-q-e-e-e-k, went the door, as it was opened. The interior was dark as a tomb. Shutters on the old building rattled and creaked. The door slammed behind the motley group, echoing through the great empty rooms. Little people dashed back and forth across the room, some of them brave, others pretending to be. The ghost dashed off down a long spooky corridor toward the kitchen. The goblins were fast on its heels. Through the swinging doors they fled and ran headlong into a huge black animal whose eyes shone in the darkness and who wagged its tail in delight. Buzz's pink tongue licked the clammy hand of a very startled ghost.

Somewhere, back along the dark corridor, a little voice could be heard wailing in terror, "Oh dear, oh dear, somebody please help me." Everyone ran to find the goblin in distress.

Judy, Emery's daughter, was clutching a tall pillar tightly with both arms. Somehow, visitors are never on as friendly terms with Colonel Cautley's ghost as the Rourke clan is.

"Oh Judy, you big baby," said the disgruntled boy goblins. "Don't be a scaredy cat, we don't want to go home yet, we just got here!" they protested. But the ghost shook its head and the troupe departed leaving the Colonel's ghost in peace. The witches and goblins were openly rebellious but cousin Judy was a relieved little girl to be leaving such a dark, scarey place.

They took a few turns around the verandah then went off down the rocks. The character with the monstrous stomach leaped over a ledge and landed in a juniper bush. "Ouch!" it giggled, "I didn't know that bush was there."

At the now empty Winter House, everyone took off in different directions, across the verandah and around the kitchen. The ghost stumbled its way through bushes and countless boulders around the back of the house. It came upon a wee goblin in distress. "Mommy," said Garnet's voice, "will you help me? My stuffing is falling out!"

Slowly the ghost moved forward. The wind was shaking its white sheet. It spoke not a word. Garnet took a second look then turned tail and raced for the comforting lights of our new home, stuffing flying over the rocks in every direction.

"That's you, isn't it mommy?" asked a curious Bonnie, blue eyes peering up into the ghostly face.

The suppressed laughter could be held no longer. The silly old ghost broke down and removed its mask. Suddenly the party was a merry one as everyone gathered around and Gillard, the littlest goblin with the floppy ears, put his hand in mine.

"Trick or treat!" We shouted as we neared the house. Frank was playing solitaire in the living room. He was surprised to see us so soon.

While the wind whistled around the house and spatters of hail hit the windows, Gary and Garnet lit their tiny pumpkins. We feasted on treats of candy and homemade cookies. There were shrieks of terror and gales of laughter as a funny old witch on the end of my floor mop tapped on the windows and peeked in the door.

Finally, the old ghost retired to the living room and a quiet game of solitaire. As the roof fairly raised off the house I wondered: "do little witches and goblins ever grow too old for Halloween?"

19

A Visit From Joe

"Tarnation," our old friend Joe was saying as he shook his grey cap in our back porch, "It sure is snowin' out there!" "Come in, come in!" we welcomed him. "Ain't a fit day for man or beast," he said, looking out towards the bay. A blizzard shrouded the face of it, hiding the islands and the distant shore. It swirled over the rocks, and around the house.

"Was headin' for town," Joe continued, "but it's a little thick out there." "Maybe," he admitted, "could be I'm just gettin' old. Today reminds me of the time about six years ago when me and the folks got caught in a storm."

"Remember the time?" he asked as he settled himself on the chair just inside the kitchen door. "Never was so glad to see the lights of Minnicog in all my life. T'was about five o'clock when we left town. Later than I like. And, to make it worse, a blizzard had sneaked up in the afternoon. The boat was pretty well loaded, half a dozen bags of oats in the stern and a big load of groceries up front. It was gettin' dark when we pulled out of Penetang, blowin' mighty hard from the nor'west when we turned at Pinery Point."

Joe pulled his stubby pipe from his pocket and stuffed it with tobacco. He lit it carefully and puffed for a minute or so.

"Now that's where the trouble started. The snow was wet and sticken' to the windshield. I had to keep pokin' my head out the window to see where I was goin'. Then the engine started gettin' balky. Guess the seas had stirred up the dirt in the bottom of the tank. Anyways, it was coughin' and spittin' like as if it was bein' strangled."

"Just this side of Gin Rock she cut out completely. Oh what a mess. Black out as the ace of spades, blowin' a livin' gale and the dad-blasted motor had to stop. I grabbed the flashlight and scrambled for the engine, barkin' my shin on the seat in my hurry."

"Only one thing to do and do it fast a'for we drifted up on a shoal. My fingers were all thumbs, them bein' so cold. Finally I got the gas line off the carburetor. Sure enough, it was plugged tight. Only one way to get it cleared in a hurry - blow on it. Well, I blew on it while all the time the boat was driftin' closer to Beausoleil. The west shore of Beausoleil is terrible dangerous with all kinds of rocks and boulders."

"Anyways," Joe continued, "blowin' wasn't doing any good, so I sucked on it - good and hard."

"Whew!" said Joe, "All at once it came and I swallowed so much gas I was scared to light my pipe for a week fer fear I'd be blown to smithereens. Well I hurried fast like and connected it so's too much gas didn't get spilt in the boat, then I rushed up front and pressed the starter. Off she went, first flip."

"By this time the snow was an inch thick on the windshield, so I stuck my head out the window to see where I was. We'd drifted down pretty close to Gin Rock so I wheeled out of there and headed towards Brébeuf. Everything went pretty good until we got comin' into the Bull's Eye. The seas were somethin' fierce. The old boat would turn on her side for a pace or two then come back up on top like a cork. The engine started getting hiccoughs agin' and I was hopin' she wouldn't stop there. Gendron's Channel is sure a small place to find when its dark and snowin'. Maybe its because I have travelled the channel so long, or maybe I can smell my way. Anyway, I hit it right on the button. Just as I cleared the last big swell the engine stopped again. Tarnation, sure was lucky! We'd 'a been smashed to bits on the rocky point if she'd stopped a minute sooner. Leastwise, it was a bit quieter in there and I got her workin' on one cylinder. That's how I run her over to Minnicog. Sure was glad to pull into your dock. Guess maybe that's when I got to thinkin' them late fall trips ain't what they're cracked up to be."

"Did you ever think of moving out for the freeze-up?" I asked.

A look of horror passed over Joe's face. "Might as well ask me to cut off my head as to go and live in town. Cars roarin' by. People rushin' around like chickens with their heads cut off!" He shook his head: "Oh, maybe someday, when I can't run my old boat no more and I can't see the channel. Maybe then I might. But, like as not I'll end my days on the shore where I've always been; where I can listen to the wind a-howlin' in the trees and watch the snow tumblin' down from the sky. Maybe its a mite lonesome at times, but least wise I know my next door neighbour ain't goin' to be hollerin' for fear I use his driveway by mistake. If I get a bit fidgety I can always go back in the bush and cut me a cord of wood. Ain't nothin' like an axe and saw to make a man forget his worries. And, o' course, when I get tired of my own cookin'," said Joe, with a twinkle in his eye, "I can always visit you folks and have me a cup of tea and a piece of that fruitcake I see sittin' over there on the cupboard."

So, on that afternoon, when Old Man Winter made his first journey across the waters, we sat by the fire and had our cup of tea and a piece of fruitcake while the snow tumbled down and the northwest wind roared across the bay.

20

Fall Break

Moon River

The first week of November brings back more nostalgic memories than any other time of the year. There were two reasons why the first days of November were wonderful and exciting when I was a youngster living within earshot of the thundering Moon Falls.

First, school was out. The annual school concert had concluded the six month school term which had begun May first, continued during the summer months and through October. We crammed ten months learning into those six months. In October we also crammed in studying for final exams along with studying for the concert. Studying and rehearsing for the concert never seemed to interfere with the more important final examinations. Christmas concerts, even though held on the last day of October, were the icing on our cake, so to speak.

The teacher (we usually had a different one each year) chose the recitations and play from one of the books they had. Most of us were hoping for a good part. We started memorizing our parts as soon as the teacher handed them out in early October.

Our one room school didn't have a piano but the teacher had a tuning fork. We learned several Christmas carols such as : Silent Night, O Come All Ye Faithful, Jingle Bells and my favourite, Away In a Manger. Our class was pretty smart and caught on quickly. The school inspector, Mr. J.L. Moore from

Parry Sound, told my folks we were some of the most
observant and bright pupils in his whole inspectorate.

Oh, what excitement the day before the concert! The big
boys strung white cotton sheets on a wire across the front of
the classroom, in front of the teacher's desk. The girls
decorated the Christmas tree with popcorn strings, tinsel and
hand made decorations. They strung red and green crépe
streamers between the beams with a big red paper bell
hanging in the centre. How wonderful the room looked!

When I was a kid, the Christmas concert was the one time
grown-ups came to the school. Everyone who could come
hoped it wouldn't snow or blow too hard since almost all
had to travel by boat.

The audience was never large but it was fun to see our
parents sitting at our desks. There was applause for
everyone, even the littlest ones who needed some prompting
from the teacher. When every young actor or singer was
finished there were gifts and hot chocolate for all.

The teacher wrote to the T. Eaton Company of Toronto
earlier in the season asking if they would donate something
for the isolated school's Christmas concert. The T. Eaton
Company sent a very generous box of toys and gifts which
brought a great deal of joy and pleasure to the children of
Moon River.

Gathering our gifts, lunch pails and books, we said good-
bye to our classmates. Except for Vivian and Judson Arnold
who lived across Myers Bay from us (now called Moon River
Basin), I would not see any of my classmates for another six
months.

The first two weeks of November were holiday time; a breathing spell between school and being corrected by an ever present teacher I had never met, somewhere in Toronto where the correspondence courses came from that I pursued all winter. I wasn't particularly fond of those courses. I dreaded opening the returned lessons to see the many corrections and notations written in red ink. But Mother Myers expected the forty-eight lessons, a full year's term, should be completed in five and a half months.

29 Teacher, Ms. Veronica Johnson, getting into school boat

30 Last day of the hunt

So, there were good reasons for my thorough enjoyment of those wonderful two weeks.

The second reason for my nostalgia was the hunting season began about that time. It was the one time of the year when Father Myers laid aside everything to pursue his favorite sport - tramping the hills of Muskoka - hills he knew so well - searching out the biggest deer he could put the sights of his Savage made rifle on.

With him were seasoned hunters up from southern Ontario - no glamor boys these - but hunters who knew when the crack of a twig meant a deer or a man in the swamp. Never a chance of any of them getting lost, nor of mistaking a man for a deer.

They were mainly friends of grandfather Myers, farmers and the odd business man who knew grandfather before he left their civilization for the quiet of Georgian Bay.

The days were usually quiet for Mother Myers and me. The men were up and off to the hills at daylight. They seldom returned before the sun was slipping down behind the North Hill. But our days were full of activity. Loaves of bread turned golden in the oven. Pies steamed on the table. There was the wood box to fill and, often, when standing at the long woodpile, I would hear the roar of the guns far off towards the Red Marsh.

The evenings were entirely different. They were filled with laughter, with talk as each moment of the exciting day on the hills was recounted in detail.

Supper was eaten by lamplight. And what a supper! Heaping platters of steaming meat, vegetables, home made pickles, pie and syrup, steamed pudding. Tea - plenty of it.

Dish washing was a jolly affair with Father Myers in the dish pan and many hands to wipe the dishes while Mother Myers stored away the food.

Then to the back porch to lovingly clean and oil the guns, to hang socks to dry and listen to the lucky hunter whose deer was hanging in the bush that night.

On several occasions wives of the hunters came north with their men. This made a particularly happy season for everyone. There were more hands to do the cooking, more of an audience for the boasting hunters, more card players for the leisurely part of the evening. When all chores were attended to, everyone settled in the living room and Father Myers threw a big chunk of hardwood in the box stove. We basked in the warmth until the hands of the clock crept towards ten. The weary legs of the hunters craved for a good night's rest. It was early to bed for it was early to rise next morning.

First, however, there was the ritual of making lunch. It was every man for himself. There were some amazing mixtures thrust between slices of home made bread. Jim Campbell had a passion for onion sandwiches. Father Myers liked a venison sandwich. Dave Murphy enjoyed a piece of raisin pie for dessert - a crumbled, mushy piece of pie after a mornings ride in his pocket, but delicious just the same.

Most of the hunting was on the north side of the Moon River over runs familiar to all, out by Chimney Rock, Juniper and the Red Marsh and up river at the Gorge, a deep cut where the river roared in a white rush around Horse Island.

Remembrance Day fell within the two weeks of hunting season when I was a kid in Moon River. My dad was a veteran of World War I. Whatever part of the hunting grounds he was in at eleven a.m. on the eleventh of November, he stopped for a minute with rifle at ease. He lowered his head in remembrance. He may have remembered what it was that took him far from his land of peace and solitude. Perhaps he thought of driving a "lorry" through the streets of London, England. A young man from Georgian Bay driving a truck through the streets of the largest city, at that time, in the world. He often spoke of the excitement they caused on the narrow streets.

He probably remembered the battle fields of France where he was wounded and lay there in a field hospital for nine days. It was policy to keep the badly wounded in field hospitals for that many days. If they survived there they were shipped to a hospital in England.

No doubt he thought of his good friend Obbie DeTonkey of Sans Souci. They had worked together, enlisted together. Obbie was killed in the war. Charlie Myers survived to remember his friend in the silence of the Muskoka hills.

The last day of the hunt was devoted to hard work. The slugging of the deer out of the bush took most of the day. The deer were hoisted to hang, side by side, on a log strung between the crotch of two sturdy trees.

It was an impressive sight for these crack sportsmen had each got his deer. Guns slung casually over the arm, hats at a rakish angle, they posed for the camera.

Then the packing up. One last evening of spinning tales beside the box stove. One last hour of fellowship and deep contentment.

"Next year, Charlie," Jim Campbell would say, "you have a big one with horns the size of a bushel basket tied up to a tree for me." Jim had shot the smallest deer that season.

"All you need is to get your glasses changed," someone would chide him.

Next morning the mackinaw jackets were discarded. White shirts replaced plaid shirts. Leather shoes instead of knee high laced rubber boots.

Correspondence courses stared me in the face.

"Red ink!" I would grumble.

"Not too much, I hope," said Mother .

21

Baking a Christmas Cake

Thunder rolled, lightning flashed and winter arrived in a snowstorm that came swirling across the Bay .

Early morning found snow covering the ground. Snow fell in the water making it sluggish and thick. Giant swells rolled down the gap. It was too nasty to go outside. But it awakened me. It shook the cobwebs out of my brain. It dawned on me - it was only two weeks until Christmas! Where in the world had the fall gone? What had I been doing? I stopped to think: I hadn't even finished my fall cleaning, I hadn't even baked the Christmas cake!

Then I rushed! I finished the cleaning all the while visions of colored lights and tinsel, of Christmas trees and Christmas cakes danced through my head.

That cake! I would bake it tomorrow. Long after the little ones were sound asleep, I chopped nuts and peel, cut dates and cherries, red and green. I got everything ready for the 'morrow.

When morning came everything was changed. The snow was gone. Winter was gone. It looked like April. I stepped outside to shake the mats and there was the bluejay back again. Perched on the limb of an oak tree with head cocked on one side, it sauced me. The sun smiled cheerily down on me. And in the pine tree, the south wind danced merrily.

"Go away!" I shook the mat at him. "Go away, I'm going to bake my Christmas cake today."

And I did. I mixed the sugar and butter. I added the foamy yellow eggs and tossed in the fruit and put it all in tins. Four cakes were popped into the oven. I cautioned the whole household not to bang the lids of the stove or stamp their feet.

I watched the cakes carefully. One hour, two hours then I prodded them with a straw. Then, one by one, as the hours went by, I took them out. First the little one, then the middle sized one and so on until every room in the house was filled with the tantalizing smell of fruit cake.

Despite the weather, there was a festive spirit in the air. Christmas carols pealed over the radio and four brown cakes stood in a row on the cooling racks. I glanced up from my work to find the sun had vanished. Dark clouds were rolling in from the west. The snow came gently, softly, until it filled the window sills. By next morning our world was a fairyland. Every tree, every little bush was laden down with snow. Jack Frost was in the water, freezing it out past the reeds. The wind was bitter and cold from the north.

Old man winter had arrived.

22

Georgian Bay Airways

The isolation of winter on the shore was swept away on the wings of the Aeronca aircraft in 1946. The Aeronca's were equipped with skis so that it could be landed on the ice. The pilots, young Air Force men back from the war, could land the 'planes on a dime.

Frank Powell and John McLaren formed the Georgian Bay Airways, based in Parry Sound. The service opened up an entirely new way of life for the folks on the shore who took to the air with a vengeance.

Mail could now be delivered weekly by airplane to the sparsely settled region with stops at Wellinton Welsh's on Frying Pan Island, Sans Souci, the Post Office at Arnolds in Moon River and at Johnny Martins at Wah Wah Taysee. Previous to this, the mail was picked up at Mactier by Julius Arnold, the Post Master and, later, his son Judson who carried it by pack sack for sixteen miles across swamps, inland lakes and hills to Moon River and Wah Wah Taysee.

There was a period of time at break-up season when the aging ice made it impossible to land the airplanes with skis. During this time the 'planes were equipped with pontoons and as soon as a strip of open water appeared, the young pilots were back in the air.

When I took my first flight in the little 'plane I discovered how vast our land is. I could see the lakes cradled among the hills, black ribbons of rivers and creeks and trails leading to houses snuggled along the shore. There was the thrill of lifting off the earth after the craft sped across the ice for a short distance. When the pilot banked the airplane to head towards our destination I looked down on my world and saw the familiar twisted pines, rocks and islands. I looked westward towards Giant's Tomb and beyond to the blue water of the outer Bay sparkling against the circle of white ice. It was a magnificent view!

Our children grew up knowing more about airplanes than they did about cars. They thought nothing of climbing in the 'plane and taking off to visit their grandparents in Woods Bay or to town for a dentist's appointment.

Folks of all ages took to the air. Mother Myers would hop on a 'plane to keep a doctor's appointment in Parry Sound or get her hair done at the hairdressers. Sister-in-law Gladys, from Moose Point, headed south to Penetanguishene to visit her daughters, to shop and return with a 'plane full of groceries.

Often, on Wednesday afternoons, when stores were closed in Parry Sound, a group of business men would fly to Moon River Basin to ice fish. Sometimes there were so many of them they hired a Norseman with a larger capacity to fly them in.

Myers Bay, as it was known then, offered the best pickerel fishing in Georgian Bay and the visitors joined the local folks on the wind swept bay. Holes were chopped in the ice with an axe or ice chisel, usually close to Fred's Point or Little Rock where an underwater bank seemed to make for better fishing. Johnny Longlade, who walked up river from his house pulling a little hand sleigh, was a lucky fisherman. The Cascanettes, Dions, Grisdales and Myers would all arrive and, when lines were baited and dropped into the cold water, they enjoyed the neighbourly talk and friendly banter.

Most would fish until sundown. The tranquility would be broken by the sound of the aircraft motor starting. The shore folk watched the 'plane take off and circle above the North Hill. They then gathered their fish and gear, heading home while shadows gathered along the river.

The Stinson, a three passenger 'plane was added to the fleet. It was a 'plane we used frequently over the years.

In 1948, a base was opened at Midland town dock with Jack Blackburn as manager and Bob Gillies as the pilot. Bob was a Midlander, his father was manager of the Bank of Commerce.

There was much work to do at the Sea Cadet Camps even in the winter so we grew accustomed to the aircraft landing on the ice in front of the house.

A larger aircraft, the SeaBee, which was amphibious, was introduced to the air service in the summer. It had a propellor that pushed rather than pulled it through the air. The silver aircraft was capable of handling more passengers and freight. The only problem it had was difficulty in taking off with a heavy load when the wind was light on Georgian Bay. The pilot would run back and forth until there was enough motion on the water for lift off.

Garnet was five when the SeaBee was introduced. He had trouble pronouncing the letter S. When the 'plane was coming in he would holler, "The Lee Bee's coming, the Lee Bee's coming mommy!"

It was Bob Gillies who came on a dreary November day to tell me my brother Allie had drowned the day before in Pine Lake. He took us in his flying machine to Blackstone Harbour to Allie's home to be with Kay and his baby daughter Sandra. He flew us to Parry Sound to say good-by to my lost brother, back to Blackstone Harbour in freezing temperatures and ice forming on the shore. It was getting dangerous and was time to get home.

Bob Gillies flew Glen and me home from Toronto on a hot summer day. Home from Sick Children's Hospital after Glen had surgery there.

The years sped by. The Scoot joined the aircraft sending the horses into semi-retirement. The great herd of deer stopped coming off Beausoleil and I missed them. Bob Gillies moved on. Other pilots came and went but no one ever took his place.

Jack Blackburn and another pilot, Ab Dinnin, made Frank's birthday one February, very special. The morning of his birthday Mary Paradis arrived by 'plane. We had invited our lightkeeper friends, who were living in Midland during the close of shipping season, to join us. Frank started the Scoot and headed for Honey Harbour to pick up Clifford who refused to fly.

It was a happy day. The weather was perfect. Frank's brother Emery with his family walked out from Honey Harbour. The cousins were happy to see one another and ran to get the toboggans and trays to slide on the hills.

A four tier birthday cake was in the centre of the dining room table when we all gathered around. In the midst of singing "Happy Birthday" to the head of the clan, there was the roar of an airplane overhead.

We pushed back our chairs, rushed to the large window in time to see a tiny parachute drifting down. Glen bolted out the door to retrieve it from a snow bank. Attached was a gift from Ab Dinnin and Jack Blackburn. Ab returned later, taxiing up to the shore. He joined us at the table for cake and tea but took off for base before darkness fell. It was a day we always remembered.

The Georgian Bay Airways changed our lives dramatically. Everyone was on the move. Ab was in frequently with our grocery order, mail, contractors or, Navy personnel. I flew many miles with Ab before he moved further north. One day, somewhere in northern Canada, a wing on the 'plane he was piloting crumpled and Ab plunged to his death. I remember people saying he died doing what he loved doing best, but it was a hard way to die. Ab was a good friend and a good pilot. I think of him from time to time and smile remembering the joy he felt flying high above Georgian Bay in his little yellow airplane or silver SeaBee.

There was a luckier outcome for young Nick Robertson. It was a brisk morning with a strong nor'west wind. The ice was glare from shore to shore. Nick was due in with the mail.

I stood by the kitchen window and watched the 'plane coming in fast with the wind on its tail. "Will he be able to make the turn into our bay?" I wondered.

Touch down and I could see the wind and glare ice were against him. Ice in the narrow channel between Minnicog and John's Island was never safe. The airplane's rudder was moving back and forth, a futile attempt by Nick to try to steer the 'plane away from the danger he knew was ahead. The 'plane went out of sight behind the Rock Cottage on the eastern point. I grabbed my coat and ran.

Fortunately Frank was working in his shop in the Rock Cottage. By the time I reached the top of the hill the 'plane was through the ice and slowly sinking. But Frank was on the ice, on his stomach, pushing a board in front of him. He reached the 'plane, yanked open the door and yelled at the dazed pilot, "Get the hell out of there before you drown!"

With a helping hand from Frank, Nick crawled out of his seat, out of the freezing water and they both belly crawled across the ice to safety.

We rushed Nick to the house where I had hot coffee waiting. After changing into some of Frank's clothes, his teeth stopped chattering and he started to relax.

Frank had rushed back to the crash site, grabbed a long rope, tied it to the dock and crawled back out to the plane whose broad wings were resting on the ice. He tied the rope to one of the struts on the 'plane. If the craft sank it would be easier to locate in twenty feet of water. However, the wings kept it from sinking any further. It looked like a wounded bird, wings outstretched over the broken ice.

Help came after a telephone call was made from the mobile 'phone in the Administration building. Aircraft came from Parry Sound and Orillia. Nick was whisked away, thankful to be going home. Going home alive!

For two days our front yard resembled a small airport. It was a ticklish business rescuing the 'plane. One slip and it would have sunk. Work was done carefully and slowly. Block and tackle were used to pull it out and planks were laid down on the ice for the skis to rest on when they got it up. Finally it cleared the water and was pulled by hand to the bay in front of our house. It was an amazing accomplishment under the circumstances. Water poured from the aircraft while mechanics worked on the motor. There was a large rip in the canvas but otherwise the craft was in good shape.

Our house was like a small hotel with people coming and going. Vital parts of the engine were removed and dried in the oven of my wood burning cook stove. It took hours of low heat to do the job.

"Would you have a sugar bag?" I was asked. "We need it to mend the canvas on the 'plane."

I had such a bag, fine cotton from a hundred pounds of white sugar. It was washed and in the linen closet. Sugar bags were used for many things, curtains, dresser scarfs, small table cloths, but this was something different. First, glue was applied to the canvas around the gaping hole on the 'plane, then the sugar bag was plastered on.

Towards evening of the second day, with water still dripping out of it but with all parts back in the motor, the propeller was given a flip. The motor came to life with a roar. Everyone including the children cheered. With Sammy Rowe at the controls, the 'plane took to the air and flew off over Beausoleil towards Orillia.

It was a sight I have never forgotten.

Weather controlled our winter flying, just as it did our boating in the ice free seasons.

One bright sunny day I took off for Midland with Gord Scott from Parry Sound base. Behind us was a second 'plane piloted by Mike McKean.

28 Mike McKean, pilot, Garnet and Juanita Rourke on the ice on Minnicog Bay

57 Ready to fly on wings and sugar bags

Above Gin Rock we ran smack into a heavy snow squall. We couldn't see anything which started me worrying about the tall water tank at the Ontario Hospital. I voiced my concern to Gord.

"You keep an eye on the 'plane behind me," he said, "let me know if he gets too close."

My heart nearly stopped right there. I never let my eyes stray from the aircraft behind us. Mike did an excellent job of following. Gord circled while I watched. I spotted rocks and trees below us. Waves of relief flooded over me! We were over Honey Harbour, not Midland, off course, but well out of danger. We decided to turn for home rather than back towards Midland. In minutes we were out over the Bay, landing back at Minnicog. I climbed out of the 'plane, happy to be safe at home and filled with admiration for the skill of the pilots.

The aircraft, followed by the Scoot and the arrival of hydro, had a dramatic impact on everyone up the shore, all in a very short period of time.

My world of isolation with singing winds, powerful storms and magnificent sunsets, the life I was born to, changed forever.

23

Christmas Up The Shore

It was Christmas eve. The snow swirled out of the sky to settle on my island home until every bush and tree was laden. Snow drifts on the hillside were waist deep. It had been snowing for days, a ceaseless, steady deluge that seemed endless.

I reassured the children, with a cheery smile, that Santa Claus would be sure to arrive no matter how hard it snowed. Of this I was certain because hidden away in the closet were many packages bought a month before while Georgian Bay was still open, before the freeze-up cut us off from civilization. Nevertheless, my heart was heavy. The freeze-up had been stubborn. The twelve mile stretch of water between our island and the mainland had been slow in freezing.

Twice it froze over only to be broken up by a strong northwest wind coming in off the wide expanse of Georgian Bay.

It was frustrating for us who depended on the ice as a highway to see it swept away and have the dark waters lapping at the shore. Christmas was not complete without our mail, the bright greeting cards from our friends, parcels from my mother and dad and a turkey - "the big bird" that always graced our table at Christmas.

Like the packages for Santa, I had stored in the many essentials for making a happy Christmas such as nuts, candies and cranberries a month before, while we could still travel to town by boat. The Christmas cake was decorated. The puddings were stored away and the fragrant fir tree stood in the living room gleaming with tinsel and colored lights all ready for the big day. But, to the grownups of the family, it all seemed meaningless without the mail.

For anyone cut off from friends and neighbours as we were, the mail had a special meaning. It had been a month since we had got any mail and were hungry for news from those on the outside. Eventually, on the 18th of December the wind died, the thermometer dipped and the Bay froze over. In two nights the ice was nearly thick enough to carry the Scoot.

However, on the night of the twentieth of December, the wind came off the lake again, raising the water along the shore. Added to that, it started to snow, a thick wet snow that weighed down the ice. In a short while there was a foot of slush on the Bay. Even the Scoot could not manage through such a sticky mass with safety. Fortunately, we now had a radio 'phone and it was in good working order. By sending out a signal that was caught by a flashpole at Orillia and transmitted through the Bell Telephone office in Barrie, we were able to speak with the Georgian Bay Airways in Midland. We knew they had our mail and turkey gathered up. The airplanes, small, one passenger Aeroncas, were equipped with skis and ready to fly our load in as soon as the weather cleared. We assured the airport that the ice in the bay in front of our house was thick enough for safe landing. Frank had marked a landing strip with big limbs of pine as soon as we knew the 'planes were ready to fly. Everything was in readiness but the weather held. Snow kept tumbling out of the sky until it seemed as if Christmas at Minnicog Island would be grey indeed.

At two p.m. we made a final call to the Airways. They told us the 'planes were loaded and waiting to take off at the first sign of a break in the weather but, at that time, visibility was zero. As the afternoon waned the visibility was still zero.

Finally, with a heavy heart, I donned boots and a parka. The children and I trudged up the hill where we could look out across the Bay. Somehow the walk in the clean, soft snow lightened my heart. It seemed, as we stood atop the hill, that the snow was lessening. Patches of blue sky showed in the west. I turned and looked towards the east and there, coming towards us through a clear patch of sky, was a yellow and blue 'plane. Not far behind a second 'plane came winging in with a roar. We raced down the hill cheering, our hearts wild with joy as the 'planes circled overhead. Frantically, we waved to let them know they were over the right spot.

Before we reached the bay the first 'plane came down and settled gracefully on the ice in a flurry of snow. In a matter of minutes the second 'plane settled on the ice beside it. The doors of the 'planes opened and out stepped the pilots to greet us with happy grins and hearty handshakes. Our boys hurried for the toboggan while the men started to unload our precious cargo. Parcel after parcel came out of the luggage compartment. The turkey was there with its feet sticking out of the brown butcher's paper. Soon the toboggan was piled high. Before the last box was unloaded, a great flurry of snow came down. It was blowing harder than ever. The pilots walked to the house with us, prepared to wait until the snow squall was over. The excited children jumped around like squirrels while tears of happiness filled my eyes.

Over a cup of tea, the pilots watched the weather, but it failed to clear and night gathered quickly. Finally, they tied their 'planes down for the night and radioed through to the airport to assure them all was well and that they were unable to return because of the snow. Then they took off their heavy clothing and boots and settled down to spend Christmas eve with us.

How pretty the cards were atop the piano. How good to get news from home. After the supper dishes were washed, we all gathered in the living room. The children, fresh from the bathtub, sat in their pajamas around the Christmas tree, now heaped high with gifts. The colored lights reflected in their wide, wondering eyes. The pilots and Frank stretched their legs towards the fire in deep contentment.

The radio played softly. Strains of the Christmas carol "Silent Night" filled the room. Christmas bells were ringing over the air and in our hearts. It seemed as if a small miracle had come to Minnicog. Nowhere in all the world was there more peace and happiness on that Christmas Eve than in my Island home far out on Georgian Bay.

24

The Scoots of Georgian Bay

The airplane had eliminated the isolation along the island chain but within a very short period of time the versatile vehicle, built by the people of the shore, brought us the complete freedom we had been searching for.

The Scoot, as it was called, took us where neither horse or airplane could; through treacherous channels, unsafe for man or beast and took to open water like a duck. The Scoot could be driven through ice too thin to carry its own weight.

It took us almost anywhere we wanted to go. We just walked to the shore, gave the propeller on its airplane engine a flip, hopped in the Scoot and we were off. Easy as stepping into a boat in the open season. Much like having a car in a driveway, except, it was much more complicated and dangerous to operate.

The Scoot put the horse into semi-retirement on the shore. The craft, pulling a sleigh (or a set of sleighs) could haul anything from barrels of fuel oil, building supplies, machinery or even hay for the semi-retired horse.

A means of transportation such as the Scoot had been dreamed of for decades. Attempts were made to design and build something but the projects ended in failure.

The first real Scoot on Georgian Bay eventually came into being in the mid 1930's, built by Malcom Dion of Woods Bay in Moon River. Malcom was one of the lucky people who went to Florida in the winter. He observed air boats used in the Everglades and put the idea to use when he returned home.

Modern materials such as plywood were not available back then so he built the hull of the punt with lumber, making it fairly heavy. The bottom was covered with large sheets of galvanized metal (thin sheet iron which has been coated in tin to prevent rusting). This first Scoot was powered by an air cooled motorcycle engine. The propeller had a wide blade and was carved by hand.

My parents and I happened to be watching when Malcom and his brother "Buster" took the first run ever with a Scoot across Woods Bay and up the Moon River. Off they went, over the ice and through the open water in the narrows. It caused quite a bit of excitement and was a giant step towards conquering winter isolation on the shore.

World War II broke out and with it the rationing of gasoline, putting the Scoot on hold. Many of our men went into uniform and overseas, some never returning to see the changes that would happen on the shore.

When the war ended, new materials to build with and a variety of surplus aircraft engines were available and the men of the shore experimented with both.

The Scoot became a Georgian Bay phenomenon as the men of the shore took to building their own from Sans Souci to Moon River (Pete Grisdale became the second person in Moon River to build a Scoot), Go Home Bay, Cognashene and Honey Harbour.

Each added their own design to the basic punt-like craft. But the front or bow of all of them was well turned up to enable it to enter open water from the ice without nose diving to the bottom of the Bay. The Scoots were then powered by an aircraft motor placed on struts at the back of the punt, facing backwards so that the propeller was used to push rather than pull.

An experience I will always remember was a trip to Honey Harbour. Sister-in-law Kay and I were on our way to Toronto. We were travelling to Honey Harbour with Walter Lizotte in his Scoot.

44 Breaking ice with a Scoot

Just past Tomahawk the Scoot started breaking ice, ice less than an inch thick in some places. Broken ice and cold water churned behind our little craft with the motor roaring and the wind from the propeller blowing snow down the back of my neck. My knuckles were white until we reached the Eagles Nest and the Scoot was able to crawl out of the breaking ice onto thick, solid ice. I never enjoyed breaking ice in a Scoot. The mixture of broken ice and churning water looked mighty cold!

Frank built his own Scoot. He set up his shop at the Rock Cottage, bringing most of the material in before freeze-up. It was a good project for the freeze-up period. Frank was an avid ice fisherman and anticipated being able to race to his favourite fish hole near Bone Island. Previous winters he hitched the horse to the cutter and away he went. With the Scoot he would be there faster and have more time for fishing.

When the Scoot was finally finished, he and Alex Lizotte, with a can of salted minnows, took off on a wonderful fishing trip down to Bone Island telling me they would fish until four and be home by five.

It came five-thirty and they weren't home. At six o'clock I spotted Frank and Alex walking near Penetang Rock. It turned out there was nothing wrong with the Scoot but the mild temperature during the day had caused slush on the ice. As the temperature cooled, the slush froze onto the bottom of the Scoot. The Scoot couldn't move. Nothing to do but walk home.

"Hold supper," I was told.

An hour or so later the Scoot came home, hauled by the reliable horse. Frank was not amused.

He found a solution to the problem but not until I had a good work out one morning. Dressed and ready to go one day, hands covered in leather mitts, he gave the propeller a few flips. The motor came to life with a roar. Frank eased the Scoot off the blocks he had it sitting on. Grabbing the bow to turn it around, he heaved and pushed, finally getting it around. He jumped in and pushed the controls forward. The Scoot wouldn't budge.

Frank made gestures to me watching from the window. He wanted my help. I pulled on my rubbers, grabbed my red parka and headed for the shore.

"Help me pull this thing," said Frank.

I grabbed the cold nose iron regretting not wearing my gloves. Frank, standing on the ice, handled the controls as he pushed and I pulled. The Scoot crept up on me until I had to jump aside. The thing was moving!

Frank leaped in. It stopped moving. We did it again, pushing and pulling while the motor roared, blowing the snow in a whirlwind. Every time he jumped in the Scoot would stop. Over and over we tried pulling and pushing the contraption all over the frozen bay. All the while snow was melting inside my boots and around my toes.

"We'll take it back," Frank shouted over the roar of the motor. "I'll have to melt the ice off the bottom."

"I'll pry it up while you put the blocks under," he said.

The blocks were cold on my hands. I struggled with them until Frank yelled, "Back farther, right here beside the pry."

I got on my knees in the snow and pushed the big wooden blocks with what strength I had left after the marathon run around the bay.

"Not so far," he hooted in exasperation.

Finally we got the Scoot up on the blocks and as I was hurrying to the house for my gloves he was yelling again.

58 Frank and Juanita Rourke with their Scoot on Minnicog Bay

"I need a rag," he said.

Grabbing my gloves, I picked up a little blue shirt of Gillards I had put aside for a duster.

"I need some fuel oil," I heard him shout as I was leaving the house.

"Fuel oil? I hate fuel oil! It smells!" I was getting cranky.

He soaked the blue shirt with fuel oil from the can I brought him, wrapped the shirt around one end of a sapling he had cut and torched it with his lighter. He got down on his knees and ran the flaming stick back and forth on the Scoot's metal bottom.

"I don't know how I'll get under the back."

"Maybe if I sit on the bow," I suggested.

The bow was too high to sit on so I laid across it on my stomach. I felt very comfortable. It had been an exhausting morning.

In a matter of minutes he was done. The bottom of the Scoot was clear. We lowered it onto the ice. He started the motor, hopped in and was off like a streak.

I turned my back to avoid the blowing snow and turbulence caused by the propeller. I plodded to the house, opened the oven door and sat with my cold toes in the wonderful warmth. I still wasn't completely warm when Frank was back from Franceville, waiting for me to help block the contraption up off the ice.

Frank built several Scoots over the years. The biggest one was bought by the Ontario Hydro to use in patrolling miles and miles of newly installed lines along the island chain, a service appreciated by the year 'round residents. An ice storm could put electrical power out of order for several days. We worried about the contents of our freezers - the wonderful appliance replacing the ice houses, until the problem was corrected.

It was a self-assured group of men who operated these Scoots, men who knew the ways of the Bay and the twisting channels. These men were confident enough to use their Scoots as easily as we use cars. They knew what to do when faced with breaking ice and open water, giving it full throttle, the machines roared with power to push out onto the ice.

Many of the men building and driving the Scoots had recently returned to their Georgian Bay homes after serving in World War II. Some had served four or five years. Frank came home remembering the "blitz". One young man returned with a medal for bravery, others had spent time as prisoners of war. They were young still, happy to be home. We were proud of them and happy to have them back.

There were no running lights on the Scoots as there are on boats but that didn't stop anyone from running at night. These people knew the shore like the backs of their hands.

There were some mishaps with Scoots and there were moments of hilarity.

Two fellows got the surprise of their lives one evening just at dusk as they were crossing the gap in a Scoot. They didn't see the wolf loping along in the semi darkness. No doubt the wolf at least heard them and tried to avoid the noisy machine. He didn't make it.

"What in the name of....!" the startled men hollered when a rangy, grey animal was thrown onto the deck of the Scoot, slamming the windshield with a great thud. As they told the story, for a second all they saw was a mouth full of teeth and wild yellow eyes staring through the windshield before the wolf slipped off.

Shaken, the men admitted they were lucky the wolf had not landed in the cock pit with them.

Johnny Martin from Wah Wah Taysee with his son Gerald was headed home one windy day. The ice was glare and it was before the ice rudder was added to the Scoot. The wind whirled the Scoot around and around, making progress nearly impossible. Eventually, after a wild ride, they reached our bay.

"You know," Johnny laughed, "I've been wind bound a number of times in a boat, but this is the first time I've been turnaround bound!"

45 The France family visiting the Rourkes on Christmas day

Scoot racing began as part of the annual dog derby[12.] in Honey Harbour, an event very much a part of the winter scene on the shore. Dog teams, pulling sleds, were used as transportation when the road, such as it was, was closed by snow during most of the winter.

Organizers eventually included Scoot racing in the festivities. After a few years it was decided the Scoot races would become part of the Penetanguishene Winterama.

The Winterama, like so many events of this kind, also emerged from modest beginnings. But when it attracted the Scoot races, it put Penetanguishene Winterama on the front page of Toronto newspapers. Eventually, people came from as far away as California to watch the men drive their Scoots

---

12.   Dog team racing became very competitive and for years Monica Longlade and her sure footed team were the undisputed champions.

around Penetang Bay at break neck speed. During this time the streets of one of Ontario's oldest towns were crowded with visitors but activity was centered around the dock area. That's where folks from the shore gathered once a year to have fun and compete, providing a spectacular show around Penetang Bay, thrilling the crowds with the show put on by the Scoots and their drivers. The champion, time after time, was Andrew (Andy) Roi from Go Home Bay.

Out on Minnicog I could hear the roar of the Scoots as they headed down the Bay to the Winterama. They were coming from Sans Souci, Iron City and Manitou, joining together with others from Go Home Bay and Cognashene. Later they were joined by folks from Honey Harbour and Franceville.

I only made it once to the Winterama. Rod Patenaude's daughter, Florence, from Muskoka Mills, came to look after the children. It was a beautiful day for the trip down. Giving the propeller a flip and the punt a push we were off in a flurry of snow. Once the Scoot was up to speed and in soft snow, the engine became quieter and it felt like we were racing along on a soft billowy cloud. Frank, in his World War II leather helmet and goggles, looked every inch the pilot of this wonderful machine. We had a great day visiting with all the shore folks and looking in at most of the events.

We had no intention of joining the races with our Scoot, so we took a run around the bay to watch the activity further out on the ice. But something happened and our Scoot broke down. No way home but to walk. We watched the races and then started the long, nine mile hike to Minnicog, one foot after the other trudging up the Bay. I wasn't very happy about this unexpected walk and, fortunately, the Ulrichson brothers from Penetang came along in their Scoot just as we were opposite Whiskey light. They gave us a ride the rest of the way home.

The Penetang Winterama provided a place where the men of the shore could have some fun with their Scoots but all of them knew that the coming of the Scoot was a revolutionary event, making travel not only possible but safer during spring break-up and fall freeze-up and faster during the winter. It had freed them from isolation on the shore.

When I arrived at Minnicog I never dreamed so many changes were in store for the people living up the shore, mail arriving by 'plane, flying off to visit my parents in Moon River, the installation of electricity, just a few of the most important. So many marvelous changes in such a short period of time, but the versatile little craft we called a Scoot was champion of them all.

59 Scoots at Penetang Winterama

Left to right: by their Scoots: André Roi wearing tam, Leo King, middle Scoot
On ice: Leonard Roi standing at front of André's Scoot
Man walking is Pete Le Page, owner of the *Penetang 88,* a tour boat

(picture by Bev Keefe)

25

A Flying Trip
to
Moon River

As the years passed small airplanes became a useful convenience to the shore and the pilots welcome friends. If someone on the shore had an emergency, they would raise a flag flying upside down and the pilot would land his 'plane to pick them up. Mail was delivered by small airplane. Orders for supplies given to the pilot were purchased and delivered on the next run.

I remember one trip to Moon River my friend Mary Paradis and I took in one of these yellow, canvas flying machines.

The sun was bright when Mother Myers, Mary and I stepped out of the taxi at the Airways in Parry Sound. The ice shone like a polished floor. Frost nipped our nostrils. A raw wind blew under our coat tails as we waited at the shore while the pilot, Stan King, lugged the huge black hose over the ice to fuel up the aircraft. The 'plane was to carry us up and over the hills to Moon River.

There was a moment to glance around at our surroundings, to look at the town snuggled on the hill across the Seguin River, at the railway bridge straddling the river on tall steel trestles, snaking its way past the Forestry Branch's observation tower atop the high hill.

The wind came in little gusts when we stepped forward to the 'plane. The pilot opened the door and we tossed our handbags on the back of the seat. There were no steps wheeled out to make it easy to get in so it was one foot on a small iron bar, the other lifted up high, stretching upwards and in. Then, with a heave on the hand hold, I found myself wriggling into the seat.

Mary and I chose the back seats, leaving the front one beside the pilot for mother. There was a flurry while we searched for our safety belts.

"Hey, that's mine!" said Mary, grabbing the strap I was holding.

"No, here's yours," I said, searching in the folds of our coat tails for the strap.

We slipped the straps through their catches, pulled them tightly across our lap and settled back for the take off.

The pilot jiggled the controls, the motor came to life with a roar. For a few moments we taxied across the ice. Then faster and faster we traveled until we felt a tug at the wings and we could feel ourselves lifted off the ice, up over a fishing shack, higher and higher until the big gasoline storage tanks at Parry Harbour looked like mushrooms.

We craned our necks looking at the Scoot tracks on Five Mile Bay, at the tree fringed lakes that dot the countryside. The belts held us down and the roar of the engine kept talk at a minimum. But we pointed here and we pointed there as we skimmed over the treetops.

"Look!" I hollered, straining on my belt, "there's Giant's Tomb away down there and there's the tip of Christian Island."

"There's the outline of Minnicog," I said, "and right down there is Moon River."

"No!" said Mary, "not already!"

We were excited and happy as the plane tilted and we circled Woods Bay. Mary's blue eyes sparkled and I was fairly bursting, thinking of the five-day holiday that lay ahead of us.

Our homes, the piles of dishes and the many household chores were behind us. As the little airplane rushed down and touched the ice we threw aside our belts, waiting for it to come to a halt.

Father Myers, who had preceded us an hour earlier, waited at the shore to greet us, surrounded by the heap of baggage and groceries. Chips of ice were scattered over the ice and up on the dock and water gurgled up through the newly opened water hole.

"Everything all right?" mother asked when we tumbled out of the plane.

"OK!" said father.

Each of us grabbed a bag as we passed the heap on the ice and lugged it up to the house. The doors were standing wide open to let fresh air into a house that had been closed up since late fall when Mother and Father Myers had left it before the freeze-up. Dad had the fires roaring and he promised it would be warm in the house before bedtime.

We made a path in the crisp snow as we went back and forth, carrying the boxes from the shore. The sun was disappearing behind the tree tops when we closed the door and took off our caps and gloves. We stood with our backs to the roaring fire in the cook stove and sipped a cup of tea. Gradually, we could feel the frost leaving the air. We discarded our coats and then our extra sweaters by supper time as the house became warm and cosy. We gathered in the living room after the few dishes were done and talked far into the night.

Needless to say, we slept late the next morning. I was wakened by the rattle of dishes and the tantalizing smell of coffee. Sunshine was streaming in the bedroom and, for just a moment, I listened for the children to start shouting for their breakfast. It took a moment for me to remember, the children were home with Frank.

I nudged Mary with my elbow and we groped for our slippers. We hurried out of our warm beds to join mother and dad who had breakfast waiting. The rest of the morning was spent in a flurry of three women washing and cleaning. Father Myers was kept busy lugging pails of water.

It was a glorious day as was every day of our holiday. The sun was bright, the air crisp and fresh. The afternoon found us walking the island, counting the Norway Pines growing straight and tall or watching Patches, the little dog, frolicking happily and sniffing at rabbit and squirrel tracks that crisscrossed through the woods. A large track at the bottom of the island held her attention.

"My what a big dog that was," I commented.

"That", said Mother, "is a wolf track!"

And that was when we brave frontier women decided it was time to head for home.

The golden sunlight was replaced by a silvery moon. It climbed over the hill to hang in a flawless sky and cast a sheen on the glassy ice. There was not a murmur of sound to disturb the night as Mary and I stood together by the window, looking out at the bay and beyond it to the far shore where dark pines were silhouetted against the white of the snow.

A mist of snow was falling the next morning, threatening the washing on the line. We were at the clothes line tugging at the sheets when the airplane landed at the shore. The sheets were left hanging for Mary and I were soon airborne once more, skipping up over the hills towards Moose Point where we dropped down to spend the day with Johnny and Gladys Martin.

It was Saturday which was mail day up the shore. Shortly after dinner people from the nearby Indian village gathered in my sister-in-law's kitchen to wait for the mail 'plane. It arrived about two thirty in the afternoon and the pilot carried three mail bags, packed full, to the house.

The next half hour was a busy one. Letters and parcels were handed out to eager hands. The pilot was deluged with out going letters to register. He took out a little notebook and marked down orders for groceries, orders to be placed at mail-order offices, articles to be brought in the next trip. There was a constant flow of conversation.

"How many five cent stamps do you need?"

"Put a two cent stamp on this one."

"I'll put the letters to be registered in this pocket, I'll be picking up more before the run is over and then they will all be together."

"Yes, I'll put the order in for you."

"Sorry, George," the pilot apologized as he gathered up the mail bag, "I forgot your order. But next time for sure. It will be in on the duty run Tuesday."

"No wonder he forgot something," I thought to myself, "it's a wonder he remembers so much and finds time to fly a 'plane too!"

The teacher of the public school at Twelve Mile Bay and her husband were there to pick up their mail. The school, one of two that operated on the shore, was a busy one that year with seventeen pupils. The problem that was perplexing the school marm was not the pupils, it was something to do with bread baking.

When I asked her when she found time to bake, she replied cheerily: "Oh, I mix it at night and Jerome bakes it the next day!"

Hydro was a new thing at Moose Point. While we waited, Gladys, my sister-in-law, proudly displayed all her new electrical gadgets. Three of the year round residents now had electricity. Only the day before the lights were turned on at Chief Art Sandy's house after the inspector had come up by Scoot from Penetang.

Although miles from the nearest town, hemmed in by Georgian Bay on one side and miles of hills and woods on the other, with a mixture of Scoots and planes, a radio 'phone, newly arrived hydro and television, Moose Point was a very busy place indeed! At least, that is what Mary and I were thinking as we were whisked away from there, up in the air once more, headed back for Moon River where Father and Mother Myers were waiting.

26

Painting Payette's

Sometime between April and June we have a spell of weather that sweeps away completely every last thought of winter from our minds, a few days when the air is still and the warm sun is full of exciting promise.

It is then we find we have forgotten the snow banks, the slush and the biting wind. We find ourselves dreaming of lush green grass, the pleasant shade of trees and the shimmer of heat rising from the rocks.

I spent a good part of one such week painting a lovely little cottage on the point of Payette's Island. It is a perfect setting for a summer home. At the front is the broad sweep of the Bay outwards to Giant's Tomb. At the back is a deep lagoon, its quiet waters fringed with many trees, a peaceful place to be on a warm sunny day.

As I was painting the verandah (a new addition to the cottage), covering the new lumber with green paint, I glanced around. There was beauty everywhere.

In the lagoon a huge dog fish lunged and rolled, sending ripples scampering over the calm surface. The sound of the gulls filled the air. I had never realized before how many sounds a gull makes: shrill screams of joy as they hurtle through the air, diving into the water with a plop, low guttural sounds while they sit on the rocks pecking at a fish.

"Yulp, scrawk, yee...ee," were a few of the things they kept saying to each other. Down at the far end of the lagoon the frogs, hiding in the marshy spots, answered them with deep throated croaks.

It grew unbearably warm as the day went on. My shoes seemed to weigh a ton and my slacks felt like a blanket. Kicking my shoes off as I climbed up the step ladder, I laid the paint brush aside long enough to roll my slacks up to my knees. I kept rubbing the perspiration from my brow with the back of my hand. I suppose that is when I got the green paint on my face.

Growing thirsty, I padded down over the rocks in my stocking feet to the water's edge. It's a tiny bay, hidden behind the point and about six inches deep. I lay on my stomach on the sloping rock to reach for a drink. It was then I found an utterly fascinating underwater fairyland.

There were hundreds of little stones strewn along the bottom. Some were red, dotted with bits of black. A few were white. Others were grey. One stone was a beauty, almost as lovely as a precious stone. It was as black as jet and sprinkled with tiny bits of mica that sparkled under water like diamonds. I put my hand down into the cold water and brought it to the surface. Strangely, as soon as it left its watery home the stone lost its luster. The shimmer of the mica dimmed and it looked just like a dozen other stones on the shore. I dropped it back into the water where it hurried back to the bottom to nestle beside a red stone and a grey one.

It was when I touched my lips to the cool sweet water that I saw the little living things. At least a dozen tiny green snails clung to the sides of stones. Many fragile bubbles were resting on the bottom. I poked at them with my finger and they bobbed a little, but did not burst. I suppose they were really eggs of a fish or a frog. I rolled a stone over idly and underneath was a miniature fish about two inches long, with a fat little body and a fragile tail. It took one look at my groping hand and darted away to the safety of a larger rock.

I stayed there for a while, just lying on the cool rocks with the warm sun pouring down on me. Finally, I left the fairyland and, as I walked up the rocks, a gull sailed over my head, the wings making a whirring sound as they beat against the air.

Everything was still. I could hear men pounding hammers two miles away. Each time I dropped something on the verandah the noise echoed around the Bay and the sound of boats going down the outside channel seemed to be but a few feet away.

The sun was on the downward trek over Giant's Tomb when I put the paint brush away. The Tomb itself was a great mound of earth and trees floating in an illusion high above the waters on a pillow of hazy, grey mist.

The gulls, startled by the sound of the motor starting, rose in a cloud, screaming their protests. I swung the boat away from the dock, out past the ragged shoals and headed for Minnicog. I stretched my legs out on the seat and propped my head upon a cushion so I could see over the bow. With one hand on the handle of the motor, I steered for home.

There isn't anything more soothing than the soft purr of a motor and the lap of water against the sides of a boat. I really wasn't in a hurry to get home. The rush of spring work after a rather placid winter or, perhaps, the unexpected heat wave made me feel lazy.

When I got home the peace of the day would be completely broken. My home, neglected while I had been painting, would probably look like a rat's nest. And there was no one home to make supper for a weary woman. It was also inevitable that five minutes after I got home, six hungry youngsters would arrive from school, shattering the last fragments of the quiet with their shouts of: "Is supper ready? We're starved."

Of course that is just what happened. I had no sooner tied the boat to the dock and staggered to the house, trying to dodge Buzz, our big Newfoundland dog, when the family arrived in a flurry of books and lunch kits.

Frank walked quietly in behind them. He, like myself, felt the pull of the spring work. He dropped into a chair by the window and watched as I rushed around, tripping over newly dropped lunch kits. Then he asked, "How," he wanted to know, "do you manage to get so much paint on yourself?"

I didn't have the slightest idea how I got green paint on my arms and legs. I certainly didn't know how I got it on my face and in my hair. That is why, later, much later, as I was scrubbing with fuel oil and turpentine, brown soap and gasoline, I thought of a song that Mary Martin sang: "I'm going to wash that man right out of my hair."

Well, it goes a little differently with me. It is more like "I'm going to wash that green paint right out of my hair." But the big question, the aggravating one, was - how?"

27

Summer Time

Sunday, the first real day of summer after three weeks of unpleasant weather. It was a pleasure to waken in the morning and find the world bright with sunshine and a soft, southerly wind ruffling the waters.

The Bay was busy with many types of craft. The *Penetang 88*, the *Vacuna* and the lovely yacht *Oceola* moved leisurely up the channel. Dozens of outboards dashed hither and yon from early morning till late at night. Other boats sat quietly by the shoals, their occupants fishing idly, seldom catching anything, but no doubt enjoying the beautiful day as much as we were.

The children, who had grown so over the years, spent most of the morning at the beach, diving in and out of the water like little muskrats.

It was early afternoon when we took off over the rocks to enjoy our favorite pastime, a walk around the island.

It was hot as we walked through the centre of the island, past the buildings and down the old wagon trail. The puddles had all dried up, leaving brown circles on the rocks. The blueberries were just turning ripe and we gathered a handful here and there as we walked along. There were hundreds of little pine trees growing around the mossy edges of the swamps, ensuring Minnicog would not have a shortage of trees. We continued our walk until we reached the small bay on the west side of the island. There we sat at the waters edge and feasted our eyes on the glorious scenery. The water danced gaily in the sun. The full breadth of that fascinating island, Giants Tomb, lay before us with the lesser islands and shoals huddled around it.

Garnet rolled up his jeans and went wading in the shallow, boulder strewn bay. He found an old rudder off a dinghy and a piece of iron of unknown purpose.

Buzz, hot and panting, waded out beside him and flopped down into the cool, clear water until only her head was sticking out.

From this delightful spot we followed the shore until we came to the pear tree Glen had discovered the previous fall. A wren sang his song as we approached. We answered his call and soon he came flitting out of the woods and into a tree close by. So easily did the boys learn to imitate its call I spent the rest of the afternoon wondering which notes were the wren's and which were my son's.

Blackberry briars tore our legs as we crossed the marsh and the hay was up to our waists. A carpet of soft brown pine needles in a shady nook was a welcome sight when we climbed out of the marsh. We collapsed on the needles and spent a quiet half-hour watching the antics of Mickey, the pup, trying to catch Buzz's great pink tongue as she lay panting after the long run in the woods.

We were reluctant to leave the quiet spot but it was nearing supper time and, even on the day of rest, appetites must be satisfied.

It was after the evening meal, when the dishes were stacked in the cupboard, that the children pleaded with me to make one more excursion. They had been wanting to see the baby gulls at Sea Gull Rock and now was the hour as far as they were concerned.

Oh, how the parent gulls protested our arrival. They wheeled and screamed over the rock as we landed the boat. Small grey eggs, spotted with dark brown and about the size of a pullet's egg, lay in groups of two and three on little bits of moss and grass, here and there, all over the rock. The baby gulls were hidden in the numerous crevices and under the ledges of rock.

One tiny fellow, just hatched that day, snuggled beside two eggs in the shallow nest. It was a sweet, fluffy chick, much like a duckling in appearance. There were others much larger but still covered with soft down and brown speckled feathers, with wings fully developed, ready to fly. As the parent gulls whirled and swooped low over our heads, we stopped to pet the little gulls. These are not the large herring gulls that nest farther out on Georgian Bay, but the small common Tern with red bill and small graceful body.

We didn't want to disturb the gulls for too long so we got into the boat and headed towards home. It was a warm, pleasant evening with grey clouds, tinted a soft pink around the edges, holding a promise of rain for tomorrow.

28

Mary, Me and a Boat

I have driven a boat since I was knee high to a grasshopper. At nine years old I was running around Moon River in the *Twilight*, a little boat grandfather Myers built. I could flip the flywheel, pull up the timer and go off down the winding river just as well as my brother. Since then I have driven boats hither and yon up the shore without once touching a propeller to a shoal. The *Bonnie-Gail*, our big motor launch which had replaced the *Minnicog*, answered to my touch like a kitten and yet, every time I set out for town without Frank, I could almost see the butterflies fluttering around in his stomach. It's not that he didn't have faith in my ability to handle a boat. I knew he was confident of my seamanship. Nevertheless, he worried when one of "his" boats was in someone else's hands.

One fall there was a smart little twenty-footer to be taken to Penetang for winter storage. If Frank took it down he'd be stranded there[13.]. There was one logical answer to the problem. I was elected to deliver the boat and Frank would go down by car from Honey Harbour to pick me up.

Everything was settled on Sunday night. When the children left for school next morning, when the dishes were done and the beds all made, I would take off with the little boat. I had done it before and loved it. I persuaded Mary Paradis from the lighthouse to accompany me.

It was when we wakened Monday morning to hear a brisk wind stirring the trees that the jitters set in. That was

---

13.   I did not learn to drive a car until a few years later.

when the butterflies started flipping in Frank's stomach. He had me out of bed before the sun. The children were chased from their beds an hour before it was necessary. "Hurry up, get your breakfast. Your mother has to get going," said Frank. "It's starting to blow out there pretty hard."

Everyone bolted their breakfast. Gillard, our littlest one, fumbled with his shoe. It was plain to see both his eyes were still not open. No one paid attention to the sun as he pushed his red face above the trees. The water scampered happily as the south wind chased it across the Bay. Everything about the morning held promise of a good warm day.

The children left with the usual flurry of "good-byes" and "where's my books?" Frank watched them depart in the Fisher and then started looking for his coat and cap.

"I'll go down and get the motor heated," he told me, just as I started washing dishes.

It's amazing how much work there seems to be when it has to be done in a matter of minutes. I could hear the motor roaring as I stacked the dishes in the cupboard. I dashed for the bedrooms to hurriedly pull the covers over the beds. Finally I grabbed my red purse with one hand and Snowball the cat with the other. I dropped the cat in the porch with an apology for waking it so suddenly. I told Buzz she must stay home and I took a look at the morning. It was heavenly.

Frank met me half way up the path with that, "Will you never get going?" look in his eyes. He didn't seem to notice that I was pulling on my jacket as I walked. I didn't notice I was putting it on inside out.

"Now, I'll show you what to do," said Frank as we got into the boat. "There's the key and that's the starter. You'll have to race the motor to get the water through."

I turned the key and pushed the starter button. The motor came to life with a roar. I raced the motor, once, twice, three times until Frank shook his head. The water was blowing and blubbering through the exhaust.

"She's slow on the clutch, so take it easy when you go into the dock," Frank said as he untied the lines. "I'll watch until you leave the lighthouse," he shouted as I backed out from the dock.

I was happy to be away - happy to be on my own at the wheel of the smart little boat. I turned its nose on Gendron's Channel. I didn't look back. I knew where Frank was. He would be standing on top of the highest peak of rock, watching closely as I headed into the fresh morning breeze.

The little craft was sleek and fast. It skipped along at 30 miles an hour, hopping over the waves like a jack rabbit. In a matter of minutes I was pulling into the dock at Brébeuf.

"Mary's nearly ready, " Cliff told me as he caught the bow line.

The wind was sending choppy little waves against the dock. The boat bobbed up and down as I shut off the engine.

"I'll let her hang off the end," Cliff said, as I climbed out, "Then she won't get rubbed."

"You're an early bird," Mary commented as I walked into the cosy kitchen at the lighthouse.

"Well, Frank was afraid it might blow hard," I explained as she scurried around gathering up various pieces of wearing apparel.

"It's not going to blow," Cliff informed me, fussing with the coffee pot. "It's going to be hot today."

"Just like summer," Mary said as we left the kitchen to walk down the board walk past the boathouse. "We'll roast in town waiting on Frank," she went on as we walked out on the dock.

"Watch for the water to come out," I asked Cliff, when I pressed the starter.

Cliff got down on all fours on the dock and watched patiently while I raced the motor.

"O.K," he said waving his hand.

"It's nice and comfortable here," he yelled throwing the line into the boat, "I think I'll sit here and watch until you turn Pinery Point.

Neither Mary nor I looked back. We smiled instead as we raced away towards Penetang. We knew what was behind us, two men perched on pinnacles, one atop a high rock on Minnicog, the other on the dock at Brébeuf, watching, with mixed feelings, the little white boat until it was a mere speck turning the red buoy at Pinery Point.

29

Myers of Moon River
A Short History

William Myers, my grandfather, was the first permanent settler in Moon River. He was born near Wilkesport, in southern Ontario, on January 28 1868. He married Elizabeth Palmer in 1886. William Myers family had been United Empire Loyalists.

In the late 1800's Bill Myers left Wilkesport in a sailboat which he built himself and sailed up Lake Huron, across Georgian Bay to Moon River. He spent several months away from his family trapping. The forest was filled with fur bearing animals - beaver, muskrat, mink and fox. Large herds of white tailed deer roamed the hills, providing plenty of fresh meat and the river and Bay teamed with fish. That was also the era on the shore when the lumber companies were harvesting the great stands of white pine from the islands and mainland.

Bill Myers returned many times to the shore to trap and hunt and decided he and his family were going to live permanently in the wilderness he loved. In the spring of 1895 he chose a home site beside Six Mile Creek where it empties out of Healey Lake into the Bay. He cut his own trees, made logs and built a snug home for his family. In early fall he stored his tools in the cabin and sailed south to get his family and household goods.

It was late fall when the Myers family set sail from Wilkesport in southern Ontario with their two daughters, Clara six, Nancy four and their son Charles, age two.

They sailed up the St. Clair River into Lake Huron where they encountered heavy weather. They stopped at Sauble Beach, a sparkling strip of sand reaching from Oliphant to Kincardine, pitched their tent and stayed there for a couple of days to dry their clothing and to bake bread.

Breaking camp, they sailed to Oliphant, a small fishing station. They decided to portage over the Bruce Peninsula rather than taking the chance of hazardous waters around Cove Island and Tobermorey. The boat and possessions were loaded on an Ox cart and pulled across to the village of Wiarton on the Georgian Bay side.

They made a stop-over at Midland to buy supplies. Bill had to go up town and buy Elizabeth a pair of shoes before she could go shopping as the shoes she had left home with were ruined by the rain and water. After the supplies (which cost $5.00) were loaded into the boat, they set sail for their new home in Moon River. To their dismay and anger they found their home had been taken over by squatters! Bill Myers had failed to register his land claim before leaving to get his family. After he set sail for southern Ontario, the Sweet family had moved into his cabin. "Squatters rights" were the rule of the times. The Sweet family refused to move out. At first they even refused to give grandfather his tools until he threatened them strongly.

Bill faced a terrible dilemma! Winter was on the way and he had no home for his three small children and his wife who was with child. Bill Myers was filled with outrage that lasted a lifetime. He never forgave the Sweets, never stepped across the threshold of a Sweet home and they were never welcome in his home all the years that he lived.

There was no way of returning to southern Ontario that late in the year. So, taking his family, he sailed his boat upriver to a clearing on the north side, facing the mighty Moon Falls. He pitched his tent and, when the snow came, he banked the tent with snow to make it as warm and comfortable as possible. On December 21, Elizabeth gave birth, in their tent, to a daughter named Rena.

The family survived the winter, partly because they made friends with the Indians from Moose Deer Point. They taught Bill many things about living on the land, including tanning deer hides for clothing and moccasins.

In the spring Bill chose a site for the home he intended to build, claiming lots 35 and 36 on each side of the river where it empties into the Bay and, this time, he registered his claim. He built a large house, which included a verandah, with hand hewn shingles for his roof.

Bill Myers made the acquaintance of the American tourists as they came to occupy the islands of Moon River, Judge Pollock, Justice VanDevanter and Senator Flynn. He looked after their properties and my grandmother did their laundry. Bill expected his wife to pull her own weight when it came to making a living. They went fifty-fifty on buying the winter supplies. She took the end of the cross cut saw when they cut wood and she waded waist deep in the water when they "picked" the logs that escaped the booms when the tugs towed the winter's harvest of pine to the mills.

48 William Myers pioneer log home in Moon River

When his son Charlie was nine years old, Bill Myers told him he had kept him long enough. So, the little boy walked down river to the Bellmoral Hotel which was built and owned by the Crawford family to accommodate lumbermen and summer tourists.

Mrs. Crawford took young Charlie in and he earned his room and board as chore boy for the hotel.

In 1916 Charlie joined the army, going overseas as a lorry driver. He was badly wounded on the battlefields of France. He was twenty-three years old. His life hung in the balance for nine days as he lay in a field hospital. Once it was certain he would survive, he was shipped to a hospital in England. During his convalescence he took some leave and went to Scotland.

One evening, Euphemia Tait, who worked in the post office in Jedburgh, was walking across the town square with a girl friend when she noticed a Canadian soldier standing by a lamp post. She told her girl friend, "That Canadian soldier looks lonesome. I'm going to speak to him." Much to the surprise of her friend, she did. Six months later they were married. It was a fine military wedding. I still have the silver service presented to them by my dad's regiment.

He was not physically fit to return to France so Charlie Myers spent the rest of the war in Scotland with the "Forresters," an army brigade which cut trees on the estates of the wealthy landowners to be used in the war effort.

When the war ended, Charlie brought Euphemia and son, Alex (Allie), named after his Scottish grandfather Alexander, to Canada. They crossed the Atlantic on the ship *Magantic* and Euphemia was sea sick the entire seven days aboard ship, perhaps with good reason as she was expecting a second child in December. They landed at Montreal and took the train through to Parry Sound. From there they travelled to Sans Souci on the steamer, the *City of Toronto*.

Charlie had left the little boat *Twilight* with some friends in Sans Souci. Euphemia, in her silk dress and fancy, big brimmed hat, my brother and their big sea trunk containing Mother's dishes, linens, and clothing, were put aboard the *Twilight* and they headed down the North Channel to Moon River. The distance seemed a long way to Euphemia. Every so often she would ask Charlie, "How much farther?" His reply was always, "Just around the bend." She said she never went around so many bends in all her life!

Bill Myers didn't exactly welcome Charlie's wife with open arms. To him, she was a foreigner. She always remembered the date of her arrival in Moon River. It was the 19 of August, 1919, her birthday and not a happy birthday either. In November, Charlie took her and Allie to his sister Clara's home in Victoria Harbour. On the 29th of December, Euphemia gave birth to a fat little baby girl. Euphemia chose the baby's first name - Juanita and Charlie chose the second name, Florence. As a result, my grandparents, Bill and Elizabeth, called me Florence while everyone else called me Nita. When we were older, Allie shortened it to "Neets."

When I was six weeks old, my dad loaded us onto the train for Footes Bay. From there we travelled into Moon River over the hills and frozen lakes by horse and sleigh.

Grandfather didn't appreciate a crying baby in his house so he moved into his workshop. As soon as the river opened, my father moved us down to the Bellmoral Hotel, the same hotel where he had gone for shelter when he was a boy. We stayed at the hotel until he had our house built on the south side of the river, across from my grandparents. The lumber, freshly cut, opened up some cracks wide enough for the mosquitos to fly through. Mother Myers soon fixed that by wallpapering the interior. She made dainty curtains from sugar bags and my dad hung a baby swing from the bough of a pine tree for me to sit in. A garden was planted, farm animals bought and my mom settled into making a pleasant life for us all in the "backwoods of Canada."

When I was five, my grandparents moved down river to a house which was on the Flynn property. My dad then moved our house to the river's edge on skids, loaded it on a scow

and moved it across to where my grandparents had
pioneered. Unfortunately, he did not cherish the beautiful
pioneer home built by my grandfather, turning it into a barn
and it slowly deteriorated.

I had a wonderful childhood. The cookie jar was always
full. I had animals for constant companions, the glory of the
Falls in the full spring flood and the excitement of the river
drives when the winter's cut pine came tumbling over Moon
Falls and filled Myers Bay from shore to shore.

We had plenty of time to skate and ski in the winter and
swim and canoe in the summer. One of my happy memories
is Allie and me skiing in the moonlight and hearing the eerie
sound of a wolf pack howling back over the North Hill.

49 The *Juanita* built by William Myers for his son Charlie (standing on deck)

When the tourists came in on the first of July, we could look forward to Judge Pollock and his guide coming up the river each morning to fish in a deep hole for catfish.

Charlie Graves was the first to have an outboard motor in the area. What a noisy contraption it was too! In those days, each tourist family had a guide; someone to fill the ice boxes from the ice house, to keep the wood box filled and the fireplace going, to take them fishing and drive the big launch when they went to Parry Sound.

When I was twelve, my mother was persuaded to cook for Dr. and Mrs. Faust. We spent the summer on Fritz Island. I remember well my dad milking the cow which Dr. Faust rented from the Arnolds family for the summer and the Jennings family coming over in the evening to get fresh milk. Allie went to work for the Jennings family and I got acquainted with the tourist kids. Lucille Jennings and I became close friends and had a great time learning to run the outboard motor, swimming and canoeing. Once or twice during the summer season, the Faust and Jennings families along with mom, dad and me, went on picnics together. Mrs. Faust had the best fruit salad I've ever tasted! Doris Faust introduced me to make-up one day when everyone was away from the island. I can still see the look of astonishment on my mother's face when I met them at the dock wearing lipstick.

I shocked her and many other people by marrying very young. But I married someone who loved me and loved the Bay as I did and we had a fabulous and happy life together on the islands of Georgian Bay.

Allie joined the Royal Canadian Air Force during World War II. After training in Manitoba, he was sent overseas. While stationed in or near Bournemouth, England, he met Kathleen Head. They were married in the autumn of 1944 and honeymooned with mother's people in Scotland. When the war came to an end, Allie returned to Moon River and Kay followed five months later. Everyone was very excited! What a contrast in welcome Kay received compared to the one Mother Myers received years before!

On June 29,1948, Allie and Kay's daughter, Sandra Anne Myers, was born in the hospital in Parry Sound, five years after Allie and Kay were married. Allie fell in love with his baby girl the moment he saw her. Little did he know when he brought her home to Moon River that he would not live to see her grow up. Five months later, in the cold of an early morning, November 15, Allie was taking some men hunting. Somehow the boat capsized. Allie didn't make it to shore. He drowned in Pine Lake. He was thirty-three years old.

I have given you this little capsule of the life of my family settling the shore to let you see that strong people built this nation of ours. They lived through those hardships just such a little while ago - the days of my own memory ago. But they did more than survive, they gladdened in the beauty and bounty of Georgian Bay and left me a legacy of love for this majestic land that I know continues both in my own children and theirs and I hope it does in yours as well.

30

Burnt Beans and Puppies

How many things can go wrong in one day? That is what I kept wondering one summer day.

The day started out quite normally, a little above average really. The sun was warm, and a fresh breeze had swept away the bothersome humidity. The children were off to school and Frank and the hired men were busy at their work.

I was hurrying through the breakfast dishes when things started to go wrong. I wanted to go and check a cottage before the owner and family arrived for the weekend and I had to make sure dinner would be ready for the menfolk too.

When I gave the sink a last wipe with the dishcloth, I decided to put some beans on to cook while I made the beds.

I had just popped the pressure cooker on the stove when Buzz started barking. I glanced out the window to see the refrigerator repair man coming up the path. We had been expecting him all week to look at Echlin's refrigerator which had developed mechanical difficulties.

"Is Frank in?" he asked. "No, but he said I was to go with you," I replied as I grabbed my jacket off the hook.

Shortly, I was heading for Echlin's cottage in a boat loaded with tanks and equipment. Just as we were approaching the dock, a terrifying thought crossed my mind. I had left the pressure cooker on the stove - with the burner turned on high.

I didn't know what to do. How I wished I had brought my own boat, then I could have scooted back and removed the worry from my mind.

The following hour was unpleasant as I visualized a hole in the ceiling of my kitchen. I could see beans all over the floor and the stove, in the curtains and on the wall.

I was happy to see the repair man putting the 'fridge back together. He reassured me, as I locked the door, that it would work fine. At least that was one worry off my mind.

The trip home seemed to take forever. When we arrived, I leaped onto the dock, said a hurried goodbye and raced up the hill towards the house and my pressure cooker. As I reached the top I was hit by one hundred and fifty pounds of joyful dogs which sent me sprawling over the rocks.

I didn't take time to examine my skinned knees, I just scrambled to my feet and kept on going, followed by two surprised looking dogs, Buzz and Mickey, the spaniel puppy.

When I opened the door I was greeted by an aroma of burnt beans. At a glance I was relieved to see I hadn't turned the pressure down, so had been saved from something worse than burnt beans.

I pushed the cooker off the stove and, while I was waiting for the steam to subside, there was a terrific crash in the pantry. Mickey had upset the bread box and was greedily devouring its contents. Needless to say, that pup went out the back door in a hurry!

I salvaged enough beans to bake for dinner. I skimmed them off the top of three inches of burnt ones. There certainly was no time left by then to go and check the cottage before dinner so I put it off until afterwards.

Before I knew it the men were in, hungry as usual and not one asked me what the queer smell in the house was.

Once again I found myself doing dishes. I was scrubbing the burnt bean pot when I heard someone calling my name. I poked my head out the door to see Frank standing on the main "jetty."

"You forgot to paint the back seat of the Fisher," he was shouting, "you'd better do it right away."

I nearly collapsed. One more delay! Of all the stupid things to do. I had worked all week on that boat, scraping, sanding, varnishing, painting and I had forgotten the back seat!

I said nasty things about myself as I walked to the boathouse for the paint. I told the dogs all about it as they followed behind. I kept wondering what else could happen to me that day.

I finally got in the outboard and made my delayed trip to check the cottage. I was relieved to see everything was perfect there. I checked the 'fridge and opened the windows, satisfied that everything was in readiness for their arrival.

The outboard skipped merrily over the waves as I hurried home. The wind blew my hair topsy-turvy and the sun felt good on my face. Buzz greeted me, her great bushy tail wagging happily. When I shut off the motor I could hear the yelping and howling of the pup, Mickey. "Mickey," I called as I tied the boat. Louder wails greeted me. I looked around. He was nowhere in sight but, by the noise he was making, I knew he was in trouble.

I kept walking back and forth searching when, suddenly, the barking was right under my feet. I got down on my hands and knees and peeked down a crack. There stood poor Mickey, on a crib up to his little tummy in water with a loose two by four across the back of his neck. It looked like he had fallen into the slip and the only way he had to save himself was to crawl out on the crib.

I coaxed the little fellow. I couldn't reach him from any side. Mickey was stuck. I looked around for something to pry up a plank from the dock and found a pick axe. I stuck the sharp point under the plank and heaved. Up popped the plank. I reached in and lifted a very frightened and bedraggled puppy out of the crib. "Surely," I thought as I cradled him in my arms, "you won't get into any more mischief today."

Everything went fine after that. At least until much later in the day. The children came home from school. We all had supper in much the same fashion as any other day.

It was a lovely evening. For the first time in a month we decided to go visiting - we wouldn't stay long, just drop in and say "hello" to our friends.

But it didn't happen that way. It was 'nigh on to midnight when we loaded the children in the boat and headed for home. It was pitch dark and a light rain hit the windshield of the *Bonnie-Gail*, but things went fine until we were in the boathouse. We hadn't brought a flashlight so Frank groped around in the dark until he found the light switch. The bright light blinded us as it came on. I helped our little sleepy heads out of the boat and guided them off the dock to shore. Frank, standing by the light switch, had to turn it off and then find his way past the slip and on to shore as best he could.

As I walked up the path holding our littlest one's hand, I remembered that Gary had, just that day, torn the planking off the bridge across the creek. It had grown rotten and had to be replaced.

"Watch!" I cautioned everyone, "There's no plank on the bridge."

Slowly we moved forward until we came to the creek with only the stringers of the bridge left to cross on. Not one of us could see them clearly enough to walk over so there was only one thing to do. Momma and Papa Rourke and all the little ones got down on all fours and crept slowly across the stringers, carefully avoiding a midnight plunge into the murky creek.

31

Remember Fall Up The Shore

A letter from Mother Myers. She was telling me of the ending of the summer season that year.

The bay is quiet to-day. A grey haze lies over the water. It clings to the shore blending amongst the trees. Overhead the sky is overcast with heavy, dark clouds. The trees, gradually changing colors, are standing still.

It is a quiet day as though our world is resting, preparing itself for a storm that is threatening, waiting for the wind and the rain.

This is the time of the equinox, when the sun crosses over the equator making our nights a little longer, leading first into fall then winter.

Although the summer people, the cottagers, had returned to their homes in Toronto, Kitchener, Fort Wayne Indiana and as far south as Oklahoma, the season's work for Father and Mother Myers was not over. There were cottages to close, repairs to make, dock work and painting to be done.

At one time closing up was simple. The shutters were put on, a key was turned and that was that.

As modern conveniences came to the shore there was much more to do at close up time. Plumbing had to be hooked up, pipes and tanks drained until not a drop of water was left to freeze and cause a pipe to burst. Refrigerators needed to be defrosted and wiped dry and the door left open slightly to avoid mildew. Bedding must be stored in moth proof closets, rugs lifted and pillows stored away.

The living room furniture would be stacked in one corner to make room for porch furniture, all the while knowing that you would be putting it all back in place next spring.

A variety of boats were hauled up into boat houses. There are no longer one boat families. Junior and sister each have a boat of their own. Then, of course, the larger boat for the parents. There are surf boards and water skis, a diving board and assorted motors to be stored away. Only then are the shutters put on and the key turned in the lock.

During my years spent on the shore, most of the summer residents of Moon River were two months a year people. At the end of August they left, not to return until the next July. A few, however, followed the new trend of returning on weekends to enjoy the fall. From Kitchener came the Walter Breithaupt family to their new cottage just on the outside of Captain Allen Straits. Their cottage was not closed until after Thanksgiving weekend.

The Laycocks of Fort Wayne Indiana made their northern trek in October for the pickerel fishing. They came armed with warm clothing for the mornings when ice is formed in the reeds along the shore. Father Myers would make ready a huge pile of wood for the brick fireplace in the living room and they would dine on pickerel - if they were lucky that day.

Most of the tourist lodges remained open for October fishing. If there was a good run of pickerel it could mean a full house of ardent anglers, most of them from the United States.

Strangely enough, when I was a child and the fish were in far larger numbers, we never bothered with pickerel fishing in the fall. Instead, Grandfather and Father Myers waited for trout fishing which took them out past Manitou into the open water. Around October 18 they made ready their heavy cotton hand lines with the large copper spoons and big, three pronged hooks.

23 Grandfather William Myers with his catch of trout

They left for the fishing grounds early in the morning when the ground still crackled with night frost and steam hung over the bay. Out they went through the South Channel to the heaving outer waters to troll around and around the shoals until their hands, despite woollen mitts inside leather ones, became numb with cold. Afterwards, they would eat lunch on an island, building a fire in a sheltered bay to boil water to make the tea. Sometimes a snow squall would swirl in; other times the wind would come up and they would find it necessary to leave the fishing grounds hurriedly. But it did not deter their enthusiasm for the sport because it was a custom, something they looked forward to each fall.

It was usually dusk when they returned. They never came back empty handed. When my brother and I rushed to the dock to grab the lines, it was certain there would be fish lying in the bottom of the boat. Twelve and fifteen pounders and smaller ones, more delicious eating in the fall because they weren't so oily. Dad's face always wore a grin on such occasions, although he was blue with cold. We would hurry to the house, full of chatter and excitement. After Father Myers warmed his hands over the stove he would take out his sharp knife and clean a small fish and we had it fried for supper. The others were cleaned and put in salt brine for winter use because the deep freeze method was not available yet.

Mother Myers went trout trolling on several occasions later, when my brother and I had grown up. She enjoyed it, especially the lunches in the open air over a roaring bonfire.

I never went trout fishing in the fall. I often wish I had because the trout have all but vanished from the waters of Georgian Bay.

32

Walking With My Children

"Gee mom, it's an awful day," said Gary as he looked forlornly out of the window. And I agreed with him.

Rain fell steadily, constantly. It made puddles on the aging ice. It ran off the eaves to fall smack-smack on the ground. "Whizzy," the March wind, bent the tree tops, skipped over the puddles and moved down the chimney. The children were restless - all six of them.

Garnet was in the back porch hammering on a miniature of the new Scoot in the shop that his dad built. Gail banged away at her version of "Bimbo" on the piano. The others were attempting, in one way or another, to amuse themselves.

What is there for the small fry to do on a rainy day? There are no neighboring children to play with. Books and toys were soon discarded in utter boredom.

"Let's go for a walk, mom," Gary suggested.

"Oh yes, lets do," came the chorus.

I looked at them. I looked at the weather. I could feel old "Whizzy" tugging at me. I could hear the water sloshing under my feet without stepping outside.

"Ah, come on, we aren't made of sugar. We won't melt." They were all gathered around me.

"But .....," I started to protest. Then I changed my mind, for walking is the favorite pastime of all of us .

"Where will we go?" I asked, as I pulled on my rubbers.

I was besieged by six personalities wanting to go in six different directions.

Finally, amidst the babble, I heard a suggestion that caught my fancy.

"Let's go and see the new house daddy was telling us about."

"Yes, let's," I agreed, as I buttoned up my parka.

Despite the rain and wind, it was warm outside. Dark clouds skudded across the sombre sky. The creek had swelled its banks during the night. The brown swamp water had cut a deep groove in the ice and spread out over the bay.

"Squish, squish" went the mud under our feet; "splash, splash" through the puddles on the still frozen bay.

Halfway across the bay, Bonnie came hopping back to me on one foot.

"Mummy, theres a hole in my rubber and my foot is soaking wet."

"Why, I wondered, do rubbers have to get holes in them just when they're needed most? Why do they have to leak when the weather starts to get sloppy and wet?"

"Shall we turn back?" I asked her.

She shook her head, and turned to splash merrily after the others.

Brown leaves, looking like little boats, sailed across the puddles. The rain beat down on our shoulders and ran off the ends of our chins.

Beausoleil Island grew near. Down Treasure Bay we went and, as we turned the point Gary halted.

"There it is," he said, "There's the house daddy told us about."

Sure enough. A new house. A house we had never seen before. A house built of logs, hay and mud. A big house nearly fifteen feet square, snug and warm, sheltered in the bottom of the bay near the shore of Beausoleil.

We didn't go near, we just stood and looked. It was Billy Beaver's new house. We thought how very lucky for Billy the Beaver and his colony to build their home so close to the protection of a national park! Old Billy would be sure neither he nor his family would end up as a coat for m'lady.

We marvelled at the size of the house. We inspected the gnawed-off stumps of poplar trees along the shore. Then we looked to the sky and it was no longer raining. So we turned for home, with "Whizzy" the March wind at our backs, pushing us along at a fine rate.

The trip was made without mishap or a tumble; until the last minute that is, when Gillard, the little one, made a mad dash to beat his brothers home. Not ten feet from shore he tripped and fell, flat on his tummy, into six inches of ice cold water.

With an amazed look on his face, with blue eyes big as saucers, he picked himself up and, in a very dignified if somewhat bedraggled manner, walked slowly to the house.

What happened the rest of this dreary day?

I dried Gillard from his little bare-skin out. I hung up innumerable mittens and socks. I wiped the puddles off the floor.

And the children?

Well, Garnet went back to building his Scoot. Gail took up "Bimbo" where she had left him and the others curled up in the living room, each with their nose in a book.

33

Joe Goes Over Moon Falls

Night was falling when we saw Old Joe's boat making its way between the islands. The soap-sud clouds that had filled the sky all day had drifted away and the brisk north wind had settled down. The Bay was like a great mirror, smooth and quiet, catching the dark shadows on its flat surface.

We strolled slowly to the dock to greet our old friend, finding the cool night air a welcome change after the heat of the day. We were greeted at the dock by Joe and thousands of buzzing mosquitoes.

"Pesky little critters ain't they!" said Joe as he swatted at them with his grey cap. "Never seems to be spring without them. No sooner do the leaves come out than they arrive, hummin' and hollerin'."

Joe fumbled with the bow line, looped it through the ring on the dock, giving it a tug to make sure his little putt-putt was tied securely. He followed us up the rocks, patting Buzz as she nudged him with her nose. We hurried into the porch and slammed the screen door on the black cloud swarming behind us.

"Sure are ornery little critters," said Joe, scratching his head, "not that they bite me. They got tired of the taste of me years ago." He fumbled in his jacket pocket and pulled out his stubby pipe. He dug down in his trouser pocket for a match which he struck on the sole of his boot.

"Reminds me of the time I used to be a river driver on the Moon River." Joe told us as he puffed slowly on his pipe.

"Them was great days when the Freeman Lumber Company shantied up the Moon."[14.]

"A bunch of us fellers moved in when spring came to drive the logs down river. What a wild old river she was then! She was rugged and the current was plenty fast when the spring flood was on."

"You must remember the last of the river drives," he said pointing at me with the stem of his pipe.

"I remember when Myers Bay, at the mouth of the Moon, was plugged full of wonderful timber." I told him. "I can still recall the smell of the bark and the big log jams that got caught on the Moon Falls."

"I know, I know," said Joe, shaking his head. "That falls was sure wild and beautiful in the spring. Some folks said it rivalled Niagara for beauty."

"I can still see it." His eyes got a little dreamy. "The logs 'usta come swirlin' down the river and over the falls to drop thirty feet or more into the roarin', churnin' water below. Then they would shoot straight up, caught in the frenzy of flyin' spray and foam. Then the current would catch them and send them down over the rapids. That sure was a long rough old rapids where the water ran down to that big eddy full of sturgeon at spawnin' time."

"How long is it since you drove the river Joe?" we asked.

"I can't rightly tell you," replied our old friend. "You were a lass about three or four when I went over the falls. Did I ever tell you about that?" he asked, looking at us hopefully.

"You don't mean to tell us you went over the Moon Falls and lived to tell the tale!" We exclaimed.

---

14.   Had lumber camps at Moon River.

"Yep. T'was a good many years ago. Probably a little earlier in the spring than this. That was the year the skeeters was so bad. They were jest like buzzards around us when we was drivin' down the river. We sure were glad when we hit the falls. From there we could see the bay and we knew we were jest about through. We didn't know it at the time but, when we hit the falls, we were in for the worst part of the drive. First thing we knew the logs started jammin' up in the centre of the rapids. They piled up maybe fifteen feet high and crisscrossed in every direction."

Joe eased himself in the chair and stuffed his pipe in his pocket. "We worked for three days on that log jam and she wouldn't budge. It was dangerous so we took turns going out there. If I can recall correctly, Danny Williams went out first, then Billy and Mose Williams and I took turns."

"It was the fourth day when I made up my mind something had to be done. I had a feelin' that big jam was goin' to start rollin' so I gave my gold watch to Danny, just in case I might get wet. It was a bright mornin' and a brisk wind had chased all the skeeters back into the bush. I felt good standin' on top of that big log jam. The water was rushing past on each side. As I stood there, I looked down river towards the bay where the tugs *Geraldine* and *Francis* would soon be comin' in to tow the logs to the mill in Penetang."

"I took a look around, huntin' for the key log that could set all the rest free. The fellers on shore kept watchin' every move I made hopin' I'd make the break. I can still recall how easy it was. I reached over and gave one of the logs a flip with the canthook. All at once the logs started movin' and I kept jumpin' from one to the other with my corked boots stickin' into the bark. Then they got rollin' too fast and the next thing I knew I was in the water tryin' my best to dodge the logs."

"The current grabbed me and there I went, helter-skelter down over the rapids with logs all around me. I did my best to keep my wits about me and when I spied a big boulder, I fought against the current until I got to it."

"I stood on that boulder for all of an hour, while the fellers on shore tried to get a rope to me. The water kept curlin' over my shoulder and the current kept pushin' at me. Sure was tough hangin' on and all the time reachin' out and tryin' to grab the rope."

56 Log drive at Moon Falls

"Sure was wonderful how them Indians worked to save my life. Time after time they threw that rope out, only to have it fall short and be caught by the current and whipped down the rapids." Then they would haul it back and try all over agin. I was gettin' to the point where I was thinkin' they'd never make it. An hour is a long time to stand in cold water up to yer neck."

"Finally they gave a mighty heave. The rope snaked out and I caught it with my fingers. I slipped the loop over my shoulders until it rested under my arm pits, let my feet slip off the rock and I could feel myself jest a flyin' down the rapids. I spied a log a few feet away and tried my best to get to it. But jest as my fingers scraped at the bark, it twisted and went out of reach. So I went on down bump, bump with the fellers, followin' along the shore holdin' on to the rope."

"I sure was glad when I got to the bottom and into the big eddy. The water was more quiet there. The fellers pulled me in to shore like an old dead fish. They grabbed me and heaved me out of the water. I was black and blue all over, my shirt was ripped in places and o' course my boots were all but ruined."

"I spent the rest of the day layin' on the rocks kinda recoverin' from my swim and gettin' my clothes dried out. I can still see the smile on Danny's face when he handed me my watch."

"Here", he said, "you pretty near didn't need this again."

"I figger" said Joe, with a look of pride "that I was the only feller that ever came over Moon Falls. "And", he added with a twinkle in his eye, "I didn't need a barrel to do it in either!"

34

Young Boat Builders

It was early spring when Gary and Garnet decided they needed a boat of their own. It really didn't matter what kind it was, just so it would float them around the shallow bay in front of the house; something to drift idly in the reeds and out to the shoal to fish for pike that lurk in the cool clear water.

Funds to buy such a boat were non existent as far as they were concerned so there was only one thing to do - build one. As soon as the idea occurred to them, there was a great burst of activity. They scurried along the shoreline gathering pieces of inch boards that drift in with the wind and waves. They searched until they found some two by fours and some rusty nails.

All necessary material was piled on a rock close to the shore. The project was started on a Saturday. Gary was the foreman and did most of the sawing. Garnet, the younger of the two, was regarded as a helper. It was he that ran errands, bringing whatever the foreman needed. By dinner time the boat was taking shape. It was a square stern punt about four feet long and two feet wide.

Things were going along at a fine rate when Frank came in. "Did you know those kids have my good hammer?" he asked as he came through the door. Of course I knew those kids had his hammer so I kept very quiet, slicing the bread as he shouted to them to get his hammer to the house right away. It is fortunate for the children that he never locks the hammer away. There would have been two sad boys that **day** if he had, for it would have stopped production on the new boat. As it was, he put it on the table and, as soon as he had turned the point at Beausoleil, work could resume.

By afternoon the boat was ready for planking. Gary started at the bow and Garnet at the stern. About half an hour later they met in the middle but, to their dismay, they didn't quite meet. There was a space of about an inch, right in the centre. "Oh gee," said Gary, scratching his head. "See, Garnet, we should have planked it from one end." "But," he added," we're not going to take it all off again."

He got busy and for the next half hour he cut strips of lumber trying to make them fit into the open space. Some strips were too wide, others too narrow. Finally, he drove one in and decided it would have to do. Garnet was then dispatched on an errand to the house.

"Have you any rags, Mum?" he asked. Since Mum always has lots of rags he departed with an armful and an old kitchen knife. The rags were stuffed into the cracks with the knife and over this they smeared a can of tar found in the workshop.

By evening the tar was dried and the boat was ready for launching. It was a struggle for them to get it to the water but they managed, somehow. There were shouts of joy as they stepped aboard and paddled out into the reeds .

They spent a wonderful summer in their boat. To them it was the most beautiful boat in the world. They fished out of it, drifted in it while the hot sun turned their backs brown as toast, enjoying every minute spent in their wonderful boat. When fall came and the icy winds told them winter was near, they carried it far up on the rocks and turned it upside down.

And so, in the spring, when the mound of snow melted and the sun dried it, it was time once again for the little boat to return to the water. It was Garnet who looked after it this year, he and our little one, Gillard.

It was a cool evening when Frank came in from work and demanded: "Did you know those kids used good green paint on that old punt?" "I never noticed until it was half painted," I answered truthfully. "Oh, I suppose you shut your eyes for the first half," he said, "then it was too late to do anything about it!" I kept very quiet, just listening. I had forgotten about the little boat. But the next morning, as Gail and I were busy in the kitchen making dinner, Bonnie came in the door. There was a broad grin on her face, her hair was plastered down on her head and she dripped water at each step across the linoleum.

"Mummy!" she said, her voice filled with excitement, "Gillard and I went out in the punt and when we got out in the bay, water started to pour in the cracks. And it sunk, Mummy. It sunk right under us and Gillard and I had to swim to shore." "Where's Gillard now?" I asked, as my heart took a wild leap. "He's coming," she answered casually and then went on: "when Daddy saw the punt floating away and he couldn't see us he started to yell. When we answered he made us swim back out and tow the punt to shore."

At that moment Gillard opened the door. His shirt sagged off his shoulders and his shorts clung to his legs. "I'm wet, Mummy" he told, me his eyes as big as saucers. He looked so much like a scarecrow we all shook with laughter.

The little punt came in handy another time. It was late October when the children decided they were going to try and trick their dad.

The west wind wakened me at midnight. It was roaring over the hill, surging through the trees and shaking the dry leaves in a flurry to the ground. It was coming in the open window, whirling and whipping the curtains.

I lay in bed listening to the commotion outside. The house seemed to shudder with every surge of the wind. The slender limbs of the poplar tree, just outside the window, were thrashing and banging against the house. I couldn't sleep. I sat up, shivering as the cold air brushed my arms. I groped in the dark for a warm robe and pulled it on as I fumbled around the foot of the bed. Frank was sleeping peacefully as was the rest of my family, oblivious of the raging wind.

I made my way carefully towards the big living room window. It was a wild night out beyond the panes of glass. Huge black clouds were tumbling and rolling across the sky. Rain was falling in a deluge on the lawn and the Bay - a Bay that was a mass of white combers, crashing against the rocky shore.

An eerie glow shone through the angry clouds, illuminating the island and the distant shoreline. There was not a light to be seen anywhere.

I sat by the window and watched the rain and the waves. It was our first fall storm and I welcomed it.

I returned to my bed and nestled down snugly while the west wind sang me to sleep. I awakened to the sound of the family discussing the weather.

"It's blowing too hard to go out this morning," I heard Frank say.

"Yeah," Glen agreed, "and it's raining pretty hard too."

I could hear the rattle of the shell bag as it was laid on the table and the "clink" of the guns as they were stood in the corner. It was duck hunting season and everyone was anxious to get out.

The little ones, Garnet and Gillard, were telling their dad that they would put the decoys out in the reeds in front of the house. They did this every year, hoping against hope that a flock of ducks would circle and land beside the decoys.

Later in the week, when Frank was away duck hunting, the little pranksters decided that was the day to trick daddy.

They went out in their little green punt and picked up the decoys. Quickly they paddled ashore and rushed for the house with the wooden decoys in their arms. Before I knew it, I had wooden ducks roasting in the oven.

"What are you doing?" I asked.

"We're going to play a trick on daddy," I was told by two grinning boys.

I watched the proceedings closely. One by one the decoys were taken to the shed. While Garnet dobbed them with roofing pitch, Gillard sprinkled them generously with feathers from an old cushion.

The decoys were quite a sight. They were the shaggiest looking ducks imaginable and so were the boys with feathers sticking to their hands and the seat of their trousers.

By this time the girls, Gail and Bonnie, were getting interested. To "put one over" daddy would be fun. The boys persuaded the girls to help them haul the feathered decoys to the little green punt. They climbed in and pushed off, paddling the punt amongst the reeds, trying to arrange the decoys to look natural as they bobbed up and down on the small waves rippling the bay.

When they were satisfied they came into the house and sat in a row on the kitchen table, watching out the window for the outboard to turn the point. Every sound was surely their dad and they would go into a fit of giggling and hand-clapping. But eventually boredom set in and they left their perch for the great outdoors.

They were so busy romping and rolling in the leaves they didn't notice the outboard until it was turning into the boathouse. They took one startled look and made a bee-line for the house where they once again arranged themselves in a row on the table.

They held their breath as they watched their father approach the house. As he stepped onto the little bridge that crosses the creek he caught sight of the decoys. For an instant he hesitated and the children poked and pushed each other waiting for him to aim his gun and shoot. But they couldn't fool their dad.

A chorus greeted him as he opened the door.

"Did you see the ducks?"

"Yes."

"Why didn't you shoot?"

"I knew they weren't real. I saw you playing outside and knew no duck would stay there with that noise."

"Oh, gee, we forgot." Their faces fell. They had played a trick on themselves.

So the decoys stayed in the bay until their feathers became more ragged than ever and the first ice tinkled amongst the reeds. Taking the little green punt, the boys paddled out to the decoys and brought them in for another season.

35

Rourke and O'Rourke

A Family of the Shore

Edward Rourke closed his tailoring business on Penetanguishene's main street, laid aside his big charcoal pressing iron and moved his family up the shore to Blackstone Harbour. It was 1911. Plenty of land was available to farm which would add to their livelihood. They would raise their own cattle and pigs as well as cultivate a large vegetable garden.

The Rourkes were not strangers to the shore. For several years they had spent their summers on Sara Beck Island which is directly behind Somerset Island. Ed was an excellent carpenter as well as a tailor and had worked in the Sans Souci area building an impressive summer cottage on Somerset Island for a Mr. Mandelbaum, a wealthy American. Ed Rourke's handiwork is still visible in the stone work that he built around the cottage.

It was a miserable day in late fall when they left Penetanguishene, towing a scow with all their possessions. They pulled into the Northwest Basin alongside the docks of Charlie Martin to wait out the rough weather. Charlie was the brother of Captain Bill and a log picker, a member, no doubt, of the Log Pickers Association. He and a gang of men spent the "open season" picking up the hundreds of logs spilled from the rafts towed down the shore to the mills.

When the weather cleared Edward and Mary, with their children, began the long trip in their tug boat to "Daddy" Gropps at the Narrows in Blackstone Harbour. Augustus

Gropp had left Penetang and established a mill where Blackstone Harbour met Woods Bay. The Rourkes spent the winter there with the Gropps, father and son, who "batched it." The Gropp men would have been happy to have Mary Rourke there. She was a good cook and an immaculate housekeeper.

The Rourkes built a house on the Blackstone property and the family moved in early the next year. Blackstone was already settled by several families. Pete and Fred Gregoire and their families were their neighbours and Louis Rourke, Ed's younger brother, bought the islands in the Harbour and stocked them with cattle. Louis worked at the Foundry in Penetang, staying with his widowed mother Sarah.

Andrew Rourke, Edward's father, was born in County Antrim, Northern Ireland. He immigrated to America with three brothers and two sisters in the mid 1800's, making their way up the St. Lawrence to Buffalo, New York. Young Andrew Rourke heard about a job opening for a guard at the Juvenile Reformatory Prison in Penetanguishene in Canada, applied for it and was hired to accompany a group of very young boys from southern Ontario to the facility we now refer to as the Mental Health Centre.

Those who remembered him told me Andrew was a tall man with a long beard. He married Sarah Columbus and settled on Reformatory grounds in a house still standing today. It was there Edward Rourke, Frank's dad, was born.

Living in Blackstone Harbour was not easy especially in the winter months. Frank used to talk about walking up Pine and Crane Lakes with his father to Barnsdale for supplies and hauling 100 pound sacks of flour on a hand sleigh back up the frozen lakes, glad to get home to warm themselves by the wood stove.

The years passed and Frank's sister Mabel married Tom Crawford, son of Jim Crawford owner of the Bellmoral Hotel at Six Mile Creek. That was the same hotel that Charlie Myers took refuge in as a boy and later with his wife and family.

Edward Rourke became Edward O'Rourke when his boss, Mr. Mandelbaum, tacked the O' in front of the Rourke name on his cheques. Edward didn't complain, he was glad to have work but, from then on there were Rourkes and O'Rourkes up the shore.

Ed continued to be known as Rourke to his family and friends, only to the tourists was he O'Rourke. But over the years the O'Rourke was assumed by some of his children, establishing the name.

Ed Rourke (O')Rourke had a reputation for being a very nice, kindly man. He met his wife, Mary Emery, who was a tailoress, in Penetanguishene. Over the years they had nine children. Gladys, Mabel, Sarah, Zita, Grant, Louis, Frank, Morris James known as M.J. and Emery.

On the 18th of October 1913, while Ed was in town, Frank and his brother Louis were sent racing across the bush path to get their sister Mabel.

Run," Gladys, the older sister urged, "Maw is going to have a baby!"

Emery, their ninth child, arrived before anyone got back to Blackstone. Given a hand by his sister, he arrived safe and sound. Later, fate would have it that Gladys would play a major role in raising Emery. She raised a fine man.

Three years later in 1916, the Ed Rourke family was on the move again to caretake at Somerset Island and to live in the large caretakers home on the most easterly side of the island, where there was good earth for a garden and a barn for the horses and cattle.

53 Somerset Lodge

52 Edward Rourke (O'Rourke) helping ladies into boat

Times were good at Somerset. Ed Rourke was not only caretaker, but carpenter and boat operator. Gradually he acquired other cottages to look after, many ice houses to fill in the winter and new cottages to build for the summer people.

The (O')Rourke boys got jobs guiding American fishermen. Guiding meant rowing a rowboat for about eight hours a day. Frank was slightly built, but many of the tourists he rowed around were two hundred pounds or more.

"The rowboat would almost stand on end," he would tell me years later.

There were lively, happy times for the young (O')Rourkes, skating parties in the winter, ice hockey, square dancing and card games.

Edward Rourke (O'Rourke) became very ill in the winter of 1923-24. He was taken to Parry Sound hospital by horse and sleigh but he did not survive. He died in hospital at the age of forty-eight. It was a devastating blow to the family. His son, Grant, carried on as caretaker at Somerset for a number of years but Mary (O')Rourke left Somerset two years after the death of Edward. Taking her two young sons, M.J. and Emery, she went to live at Wah Wah Taysee with her daughter Gladys who was married, by then, to Johnny Martin.

Her son Louis, Frank's older brother, took over caretaking at The Yankanuck Club until a heart attack, at an early age, forced him to leave the shore. Frank's younger sister, Sarah Garratt, took over and she and her sister Zita Grisé, were at Yankanuck for many years from early spring until late fall.

Frank Rourke took over Somerset. He and I were married and had been living at Somerset for two years when it was bought by Jack Creed of Toronto, just before World War II broke out.

Frank joined the army and, when he returned from overseas, we moved back up the shore as soon as we could, this time to Minnicog. Emery O'Rourke bought land in Honey Harbour and built it up to one of the largest and most successful marinas on the shore. And Harold O'Rourke,

Edward's grandson, established a tourist resort on Green Island.

54 The Yankanuck Club employed
many (O')Rourkes over the years

The Rourkes and O'Rourkes, one family, two names, have lived on the shore from the time of wood burning steam tugs.

Sometimes, when I head up the shore, up Sans Souci way, and the boats are whizzing by, I think of Edward and Mary slowly making their way in an old tug boat, pulling a scow with all their worldly possessions, looking for a better life for their family in the isolation of the shore.

36

Shadows of the Past

The wind, that had been violent for many days, swung at last to the south, lulled and finally died. The grey overcast cleared gradually. By evening the sky was crystal clear.

It was four o'clock when I walked down the path from Mother Myers house to the dock. I was heading home after a short visit. The leaves were wet and clinging to the grey rocks. The brown leaves still held fast to the old oak tree hanging over the dock. An outboard hurried up the far shore of Woods Bay, a quiet bay now that the summer folks had gone. Cottages, their windows shuttered tight for the winter, had a cold appearance. The whole Bay seemed to be at peace, resting, making ready for the blanket of snow old man winter would soon fling carelessly over it.

Currents swirled as we passed through the Captain Allen Straits. The cottages at Iron City Fishing Club were washed by the pale, late afternoon sunshine. No other boat stirred anywhere as we made our way out the south channel. A flock of ducks circled out of Whistler Bay.

Shadows had gathered along the rocky shore by the time we reached the Hole in the Wall near Manitou. The water was considerably lower than the last time I came down the shore by boat. Shoals stood high above the water, thrusting bold heads above the restless waves.

Darkness had slipped over the area by the time we reached the "Horn," as we often call O'Donnell Point. The sun died in glorious reds far out over the open Bay. The waters were inky black. Now and then we caught sight of the light on Glen's boat in front of us.

Glen, our oldest, after years of learning the ways of the shore from his dad, grandfather Myers and his uncle Emery, was now able to navigate the shore on his own and almost old enough to take his place alongside them as men of the shore.

There was a dead roll coming in and the boat swayed up and over each long wave.

"Look!" I said to brother-in-law Emery. "There is the first star."

He peered out of the windshield, searching the sky. "Where?" he asked.

"Up there," I replied, pointing toward it.

Off in the distance was the outline of Giant's Tomb. Nestling farther out, but unseen, were the Watchers and the Western's - small dots of stone and earth 'midst a wide, rolling expanse of cold water.

"There are two buoys just ahead of us," Emery said, "can you see them?"

I stared hard into the blackness. I have never been good at spotting buoys at night. I didn't see the black one on my side until we were slipping past it. As usual, I marvelled to myself how a "sixth sense" seems to guide the men of the shore on a dark night.

A twist of the wheel and the boat turned down the channel, safe between the rugged mainland and the outer islands. The waters were calm again. I tapped my cold feet and thrust cold hands deep into my pockets. There is little comfort on the water at night, late in the fall.

"We'll stop in at Johnny's," Emery suggested. "We'll get warm there." He blinked the boat lights three times as a signal to Glen. My son swung his boat in behind us and followed us into the boathouse.

The house was in darkness. It seemed the Martins were not at home. I felt a tug of disappointment. I had been promising to drop in on Frank's sister and her husband for some time and when I finally made it they were not at home.

While we were nudging the boats into the dock I saw lights of a boat coming out of Kings Bay.

By the time we were tied up, Ralph King and a workman up from Penetang landed on the opposite side of the boat house. They walked around the boathouse to be greeted by Emery.

"Go to the house Nita where it's warm," I was urged. I hesitated, listening to the excited barking of a dog.

"Is that dog tied up?" I inquired. I was assured that it was.

I left the dock and made my way up the path to the house. A wood fire was crackling in the kitchen stove. I relished the heat as I spread my hands over the top of it. In minutes I was able to discard my coat. I glanced around the kitchen, the very same one I had been entertained in by my sister-in-law and her husband many times before. But there was a difference. The old kitchen where I had visited since I was a child was changed. The old familiar cupboards were gone and in their place handsome, new modern cupboards lined the wall. The pantry where I have watched grandmother Rourke bake delicious pies and bread when I was a youngster had disappeared.

There was a difference and yet, in the familiar surroundings of the late fall evening, fond memories crowded around me. I remembered the days when my brother Allie and I walked across from Moon River to join in the fun of a Christmas concert at the school house. This big old house was filled with young people and their music and singing. The (O')Rourkes, along with the Martins, had their own family orchestra which included a fiddle, piano, banjo, guitar and mouth organ.

Week days were filled with logging, wood-cutting and ice-filling and in this kitchen many a hearty meal was polished off by young men and women, their appetites whetted by the crisp shore air.

Sunday afternoons, during the winter, they played shinny on the ice and came in to warm up in this kitchen.

This house and this kitchen had always been filled with life, music and family. All that remained here of that family now, were Johnny and Gladys and, for me, the shadows of the past whispering over my shoulders.

The men came tramping in from the dock interrupting my reverie. "What about a cup of tea?" Emery inquired while they warmed themselves around the fire.

As we left their home, I was sorry Gladys and Johnny were away. But I was grateful for my little visit with the past in their delightful kitchen.

I wrapped myself in a blanket for the remainder of the journey down the shore. The stars were out in all their glory. Nowhere are they more bright, more easily seen than out in a boat at night. The big dipper, the polar star, all of them were shining in the clear sky.

Northern lights surged high among them, darting and dancing, adding still more beauty to the night. We snaked our way through narrow channels where gnarled pines were silhouetted and buoys now popped up at frequent intervals. Then we were out into the open, running on the flashing lights, first Red Rock, then at Eatons Island. The waters were restless across the gap, bouncing the boat, little fingers of spray splashing against the windshield.

Quiet waters greeted us when we got home. Our families were waiting, flashlights bobbing at the dock. We climbed out. The journey was over. I stamped my cold feet while the men tied up the boats. Then I rushed off with sister-in-law Peg for a cup of hot coffee before she and Emery left for home.

My latest trip up the shore was over. I was grateful for the warmth of the coffee cup in my hands but the beauty of the trip, the serenity of the Bay, the glory of the heavens, will be a memory to cherish all through the cold months ahead.

26 Brother Allie Myers with Juanita Myers Rourke

Allie drowned one cold November day at age 33

37

To Town With the Fisher

"Remember now, pull the choke out a little when you land in Penetang or it may stall on you," Frank reminded me as he pushed the boat away from the dock at Honey Harbour.

I nodded as I waved a cheery goodbye. I felt exultant as I nosed the boat out through the channel. It was my first trip alone this year and I was delighted. The steering wheel felt good in my hands. The motor purred evenly.

I was taking the Fisher to town for needed repairs on the propeller shaft and rudder. Getting it to town presented a problem. It was necessary to leave it in "hospital" overnight. If Frank took it down there would be no way for him to get back.[15.] We did much talking on the subject. Then Frank said, "We'll take the kids to school Monday morning, then you take the Fisher to Penetang and I'll go in and pick you up with the car."

Monday morning dawned bleak and grey. Clouds covered the sky from horizon to horizon. The wind came from the east and smelled of rain. The day didn't look promising.

There was the usual morning rush. The children were now attending school in Honey Harbour and had to be driven in every day. Six young people gathering books and lunch-kits and the usual arguments as to who would sit where in the boat. The cold morning air put an end to it all as they huddled under the blankets. There was little chatter as we headed for Honey Harbour.

---

5. I still did not drive a car.

"It would be a lot shorter for you to go down through the Honey Harbour channel," suggested Frank as we got underway.

I had planned on coming back out by Minnicog and down the main channel because that's the route I knew.

"But," I protested, "I've never taken a boat down that way alone."

"I know," he said, but it's all buoyed out." He gave me detailed instructions on where to go. "But, please yourself," he said as he watched my puzzled expression.

I had all this in mind as I left the dock at Honey Harbour and turned at Trail's End to head up toward the Royal Hotel. I pondered the problem. Which way should I go? The long way that I knew as well as the back of my hand or the shorter route that I didn't know at all.

I looked at the overcast sky. I looked at the channel ahead of me and decided there was only once to learn and it might as well be today. I turned the wheel to the left. I headed down the channel past the Royal Hotel. I was on my way.

I pulled the hood of my coat tightly around my face. The early morning air was chilly. The boat skipped along at a fine rate.

A man working at Picnic Island glanced up as I passed and then went back to his work.

Through the first set of buoys we went - the boat and me. Nothing to this channel at all. But in a matter of minutes we came upon not just one set of buoys but two. Two sets of buoys with an island between them!

I was surprised. I slowed the boat to a crawl. Far to the right I saw the white beacon where I had to turn. But between me and the beacon were two sets of buoys.

Why didn't I listen more closely to Frank's instructions? I scolded myself as I edged the boat slowly forward.

Take your choice, the buoys seemed to say.

I did. I turned to the left. I decided to sneak through far enough to see if there were more buoys on the far side of the island.

Filled with apprehension, I put the motor in idle. I strained my eyes in search of a buoy but saw nothing except waves washing over a shoal dangerously near. My heart stopped beating for an instant, but my head and hands worked, thank goodness. I reversed the engine and slowly inched the boat around. This certainly wasn't the way to Penetang.

I skedaddled out of there like a scared rabbit and swung toward the right. I poked along, watching over the side for anything that looked like a shoal. I breathed a sigh of relief as I turned at the white beacon and headed for Beausoleil. Somewhere out in that expanse of water was a red buoy. Far ahead of me I could see it but it wasn't red. It was practically white. All the paint had worn off except a little on the very tip. I'm really ambitious on my first trip of the season is what I was thinking as I slipped along.

The wind was freshening. A breeze coming out of Waubaushene Bay blackened the water's surface. The boat rocked and jumped in the choppy waves. A prankish spray flew over the side. My hood had slipped off unnoticed and the spray soaked my hair and gloves. I pulled the hood back up in place and stuffed my left hand in my pocket to get it warm. When my right hand felt like a block of ice, I switched.

As I passed the red buoy I put the bow on the white beacon at Midland Point.

How far do I go before I turn for Penetang? I wondered. I didn't know so I kept on going until I hit the familiar boat channel. Ah! I felt much better. Now I knew where I was. Off I went at full speed. I felt ten years younger!

It was hard to see the shoreline. It seemed a very long way across the gap. I couldn't see Whiskey light though I strained my eyes in a vain attempt. I kept running nor'west until I could see smoke billowing up from the incinerator at the Ontario Hospital. On a bit farther and Whiskey light appeared out of the morning mist.

Two seagulls wandered over top of me. A startled loon submerged quickly a few feet in front of the boat. I watched a bus leave the Nor'West Basin and follow the winding road at the edge of the Bay. The wind tugged and chilled me as I turned into Penetang Bay. The docks and buildings were a blur until I drew close to them. Not a soul stirred anywhere.

I removed my wet gloves, pulled down the hood of my coat and tried frantically to flatten my wild looking hair.

My teeth were chattering as I left the dock. I was conscious of my heavy clothes and my wind blown hair as I walked up the street and I was not the least bit surprised when a middle-aged woman, decked out in her Easter finery, took time out from her window shopping to stare in amazement at me as I passed by. I didn't know what she was thinking but I held my head a little higher and walked a little faster.

38

Rescued By A Friend

The twenty-fourth of May weekend gave us the first taste of what we could expect in the weeks and months to come.

Water taxis rushed up and down the shore trying to keep up with the demand for their services.

The week preceding the holiday was usually more trying than the weekend itself. One year I still had two cottages to get ready, a fairly simple chore. But with rain, wind, cold and a balky outboard motor to contend with, I had a terrible time and was behind schedule. Everything seemed to go wrong.

My first trip to the cottages began in a light drizzle which became a deluge by the time I reached Tomahawk Island. The glove on my steering hand was soaked and my hand was cold. Rain seeped down the back of my neck. A mist hung over the islands and a brisk east wind roughened the water.

The cottage is a little jewel on the island and nestles in a deep bay. But, I had difficulty holding the boat to the dock. When I stood on the bow, my chin was just above the top of the dock. I struggled to hold the boat at the dock while I searched for a step to climb up. The outboard bobbed up and down with the waves. The deck was slippery. One slip and I would be head over heels in the Bay.

I rolled up onto the dock, holding the bow line firmly in one hand. The wind whipped my raincoat. My legs and feet were soaked.

I snubbed the boat tightly and fled to the cottage. I fumbled with the key in my stiff fingers. Then the door opened and I was safely inside.

On the way home that evening the weather showed no signs of improvement. Night was closing in early and, for added irritation, the motor developed the hiccoughs. It burped and gurgled, slowing down then speeding up, making the homeward journey much longer than ususal. If Frank's ears were ringing it was because I was saying things about him taking our own good motor with him and leaving me to beg or borrow a poor substitute.

I battled the elements the next day too. A high wind sent rollers big enough to force me to run with them first one way up the Bay then switch hurriedly to run the opposite way, all the while heading toward my destination, an island just off the shore of Beausoleil. The motor behaved perfectly until I came to calmer waters. Then it stopped dead! I glanced quickly at the gas tank. It was three quarters full. I cranked the motor again and again. The east wind caught the light boat and whirled it over the water. I fumed and fiddled. I looked about at my surroundings, grabbed a paddle and went frantically to work because I was drifting quickly past the last rocky point between me and the wide sweep of Georgian Bay.

Somehow, I managed to beat the wind and latch on to the point. I scrambled ashore and slipped the bow line around a boulder. I sat hunched on the shore, holding the boat off the rocks. My surroundings were familiar, the narrow channel far off Pinery Point and the lighthouse in between. I wasn't frightened for I love Georgian Bay when it is wild and rough. But I watched the lighthouse closely hoping the Paradis' had seen me. "If they don't," I was thinking,"I am in a pickle."

With a dead motor and 'way off course, my son Glen would never find me if he came searching.

I had only a few minutes to wonder. Soon an outboard left Brébeuf dock. It splashed across the gap and drew up alongside. "What are you doing?" asked Cliff. I explained. "I'll tow you around to Bev's[16.] dock," he shouted, hunching his shoulders against the wind, "and we will see what is the matter."

The east wind pushed the two boats and bounced us all around. Spray was flying. The rocky shore looked at us hungrily and then we slipped away into the quiet little harbour. The motor wouldn't start so we tied the boat up. "We will go to the light," said Cliff, "and get you warm, then we will decide what to do."

It was wonderful to get inside the cosy lighthouse. I was chilled to the bone. The hot cup of tea was heavenly. We sat by the table and watched the rain beat against the window pane. Watching the waves thrashing against the shore, we realized the weather would not settle that day. "I think you had better forget cottage cleaning for today," Mary suggested. I nodded. The taste for work had left me.

[16.] Bev Keefe, destined to play an even more important role in my later years.

We towed my outboard to the cottage and tied it securely, loaded the cranky motor in Cliff's boat and headed toward home. The channel was choppy. The wind was cold and miserable and the rain pelted down.

The Bay seemed desolate, resembling a day in late fall. The gulls were grounded, huddled together on a rocky point. I peered skyward, with the rain beating down on my face and wondered what adventure lay before me tomorrow when, once again, I would be on the channel heading out toward the open Bay.

39

Shore Memories

It was a glorious day. The far shore was smoky and the sun was blazing. The back door stood open. Many squirrels, black, grey and red, were having a heyday in the food basket hanging in the apple tree.

Basking in the sunshine that was streaming in the living room window were Frank, me and our friends, Mary and Cliff. It was not unusual for us to reminisce when we got together - to talk about the "old" days on the shore and to compare them to "these" days.

"How they get around now," said Mary shaking her head.

"When I think of the chances we took," said Frank.

"I can remember once," he went on, "crawling on my stomach for two or two and a half miles all the way from our home at Somerset Island to Sans Souci because the ice wasn't good enough to walk on!"

"You must have been anxious to go somewhere," I put in.

"I was going to Parry Sound for the mail," he replied, "and I was picking up mail at MacNamara's at Sans Souci to take with me".

"Once I got that far I could go inland amongst the islands where the ice was good and I would be able to stand up and walk from there."

"Another time a friend of mine and I skated on ice that was so thin it cracked in front of us as we skated along."

"We thought it was a lot of fun," he shuddered. "We were going to look at an icehouse my father was to fill with ice."

"We didn't tell anyone where we were going, so, if we had not got back, they wouldn't have known where to look for us."

The cracking ice reminded me of a trip Father and Mother Myers, Frank and I made up the Moon River from Wood's Bay to Arnold's who lived on Myers Bay. We followed the shore but had to cross the river to reach Arnold's. The river ice was black. Father Myers drove the horse. Frank went ahead with the axe to try the ice. He didn't chop through the ice to see how thick it was, he just smacked it every few feet with the back of the axe and kept on going. Father Myers, standing in the front of the cutter, drove the horse behind him. The ice cracked in every direction as the horse trotted along while Mother Myers and I, seated on the cutter, had heart palpitations.

"I was thinking the other night," said Frank," "about the fall everyone around Sans Souci had the 'flu. We still had to get our fall supplies in."

"When my dad recovered, he and I went to Parry Sound in the steam tug and got the supplies. Hundred pound bags of sugar and flour and all the rest."

"We stopped at MacNamara's at Sans Souci on our way back. They were all in bed with the 'flu. And that's where everything went wrong."

"There were just stringers on the dock. My dad didn't notice they were ice covered until he jumped out of the boat. He lost his footing and fell in the water up to his neck."

"I didn't stop the tug in time," Frank continued, "and it ran up on shore and keeled over to one side."

"So, there was my dad and me in the water rescuing the supplies."

"Did you ever see a bag of wet sugar?" he asked.

"It would turn hard," answered Mary.

"It was ruined," said Frank. "We had to throw it away."

"The flour bags hardened on the outside, so we saved most of the flour. We borrowed a rowboat from Fred MacNamara and rowed home to Somerset. Boy was it cold!"

"The next day," he recalled, "Leo Dorion, who lived on an island next to us with his parents, went back to Sans Souci with me."

"We got the tug righted and got steam up in the boiler, loaded the supplies back on and got them home."

"You don't have to go back that far to remember some of your hair raising escapades," said Mary. "Remember the spring you two had to make the horse gallop all the way across the gap from Sawlog Bay to Minnicog?"

"We didn't dare let him stop," grinned Cliff, "because the ice was so bad he would have dropped right through!"

"If your kids ever did the things you two have done," said Mary, "you would have a fit."

"If my kids ever thought about doing such things," said Frank, I'd wring their necks!"

40

Good-bye Buzz

Fog lay tight over the islands, hugging the Tagalders by the shore. It glistened on the pine needles. The dismal roar of the foghorn rolled across the limpid waters of Georgian Bay.

It was a mean, miserable day. Water gurgled from the eaves and washed the snow from the side of the house, down into pools of slushy water in the yard and onto the new ice. Out on the big Bay the water was lying calm and listless. The whole wide sweep of the Bay seemed to be holding its breath, waiting - waiting for the north wind, for a surge of polar air that would bring winter again.

Freeze-up was going to be prolonged. It started early and caught us all a little unawares. One night the air was balmy, there wasn't a trace of frost. Water slapped happily against the sides of the green outboard tied at the dock.

But the world we wakened to the next morning was transformed. The late flowering sweet peas were hanging limp on their vines, snow covered their roots. The window panes bore a dramatic picture drawn by Jack Frost. Bully Bluejay was in the maple tree hollering his greedy head off for someone to put out the feeding station. At the shore, the green outboard was frozen in the ice.

The next few days saw the Bay freeze farther out. Channels closed in. Everyone up the shore was breaking ice, pushing it aside to make a last minute dash to town. There is always last minute shopping to do before freeze-up sets in for good.

They hurried to town, shivering in their parkas and heavy boots, while the splashing water froze on the windshields of their boats. Their feet, clad in rubber boots, took them up the snow covered sidewalks and into the gaily decorated stores. They hurried with the ordering, hurrying so they could get away early and back up the Bay before dark, before a snow squall filled the "gap", folding around the islands like a great white blanket. This one last trip would do until the waters were frozen for another season.

Once the freeze-up starts there is only one wish in everyone's heart: that it come quickly to get the ice thick enough before Christmas so it will be easy to get out for the Christmas turkey, the mail and to carry Santa's reindeer along the rocky shore.

But the weather was in a contrary mood. It tossed its head and a nor'wester smashed the channel ice. It switched to the south and flung rain over the shore. The islands were a sheet of ice. It froze on the tree trunks, made jewels of the pine needles and turned the clothesline into a glistening ribbon. The children slid down the path and giggled when they fell.

It was a miserable, misty day. All was quiet on the shore but the afternoon was broken by a visitor. He came walking across the ice, picking his way, dimpling the puddles with his rubbers. Our old friend's parka was open, mist clung to his bushy grey eyebrows. I opened the door as he came up the steps.

"Well, how did you get here?" I asked. "In my canoe," said Joe. "Landed over there on the other side of the point. Not much ice," he went on, "but I was froze in last week." A lot of others were, too I suppose, but yer maw and paw made it out I see."

"And Glen," I put in. "He was up there with them for hunting season."

"Yer dad get his deer as usual?" Joe asked.

"And Glen too. His first." I replied with pride.

"Well good fer him," our old friend said. "I didn't get galavantin' very far this year. T'wasn't safe fer a feller to be in the bush out my way. I was out in the bush not too far from the house one day cuttin' wood. I thought I was all alone, when all at once I heard 'zing, 'zing', and there was bullets flyin' around my head like a bunch of bees. I ducked behind a brush pile and stayed there until them dern fool hunters left, then I beat it fer home and I stayed there. I jest figured it was better to kill one of my steers fer meat than to go out in the bush where a bunch of green horns with guns in their hands were prowlin', shootin' at anything that moved."

"Say," said Joe while he fumbled in his side pocket for a match, "I missed Buzz comin' to meet me at the shore. Where is she anyway? I sorta missed her hollerin' and waggin' that big tail of hers."

Perhaps Joe could tell by my face that something was wrong. He leaned forward in his chair. He took his stubby little pipe from his mouth.

"Ain't nothin' wrong with Buzz, is there?"

I didn't know how to tell Joe. It was hard for me to even think that my beautiful, black Newfoundland dog was dead. I tried to tell him how I missed tripping over her while I cooked supper. How much I missed the look in her soft, gentle eyes and the sound of her big bark echoing around the Bay.

"Gol," said Joe, "gol dern it anyway. What happened?"

I shrugged. "She was off color for a day or so. But nothing unusual. She was around me all day. She barked through the night and in the morning we found her curled up under the back step." My proud beauty would never bark again.

"Tarnation," said Joe, "Ain't it a shame."

"She had a wonderful life," I told him. "And she brought us a lot of joy. After all, she was just a ....." but I couldn't finish what I was saying, because my lip was quivering so.

I looked across at Joe, he was crying too.

33 Good-bye old friend

41

End of a Great Era

Many changes occured on Minnicog during the Navy years. Every building was restored to perfection. New roofs were replaced where needed and all were reshingled. Many coats of cream paint were applied to the weather beaten buildings. Minnicog was allowed to keep its original colour instead of the war time grey. Broken windows were replaced and the main jetty was rebuilt and enlarged to accommodate the various boats required for training the sea cadets.

George Parr of Midland installed a battery operated system, bringing lights and refrigeration to the Camp for the operating season. When hydro came aboard later, Bev's Marine Ltd., of Midland, installed individual services in each building, electrified the water pumps in the pump house and removed all the old overhead wiring.

In the early 1950's Harry Gillard, Secretary of the Navy League of Canada, retired. He had, for several years, been the one person with his hand on the pulse of the cadet operation and had become our friend. His son was our son's godfather. Then, Lt. Commander Jim Crist replaced Lt. Commander Bill Pierce who moved to Naval Command in Newfoundland as Commander. These losses of old friends were only the beginning.

In 1951 it was decided to close the Princess Alice Sea Cadet Camp. The Camp was being moved to Camp Ewing, a Navy League stronghold on the Ottawa River. We were told the Navy had decided to substitute Camp training for training on Naval bases on both coasts.

55   Princess Alice Sea Cadet Camp moves out

Lt. Commander Crist and Lt. Ken With were involved in arranging the big move. All of the boats, including sailing dinghies and cutters, were towed away and shipped out by rail. All of the kitchen equipment, medical stores, blankets, folding benches and tables, everything, was shipped out.

Equipment left at Princess Alice Camp was secured under lock and seals. Frank was notified he was responsible for all Naval Stores located at the Camp.

Eventually, certain articles were declared surplus and purchased by Hercules Sales and Service of Toronto. Mr. Goldstein sold the walk-in refrigerator to Frank for one hundred dollars.

Hercules Sales made an offer of fifty thousand dollars to the Navy League to purchase Minnicog. They wanted it for a boys camp. Due to the restrictions applied when the Navy League acquired it, the offer could not be accepted.

The Queen Elizabeth Camp on Beausoleil Island was taken over by the London, Ontario Y.M.C.A., May 1954.

On April 22, 1955, the Navy League of Canada sold Minnicog to Margaret Wallace Jarvis for one dollar.

Some people believe that the old buildings on Minnicog were burned. That is not true. I was there and saw them torn down or moved. The facts are as they are presented here.

The new owners of Minnicog made an agreement with the Cumming Brothers of Midland, formerly Webb and Cumming, to tear down or remove all buildings except the boat house, the Green Cottage, Winter House, Pump House, and the house that had been built for us to live in. In return, the Cumming Brothers retained all rights to the contents and materials from the buildings they tore down.

The Cumming Brothers, Bill and Ike had been involved in construction for many years. They had done the refitting of Minnicog for the Navy League of Canada and were pleased now at getting this lucrative contract to clear it out. At the time they were building cottages near by for Lt. Colonel Stuart Bates on Pincushion Island, directly east of Minnicog and a cottage for H.W. Peplar on an island Nor'westerly of Thibodeau Island. Colonel Bates was anxious to have the tall doors from the Officer's Mess in the main building installed in his cottage.

We purchased the Rock Cottage and Cook's quarters, including any furnishings, from the Cumming Brothers for four hundred dollars. The Rock Cottage was moved to Gendron's Channel and survives to this day. It is where I now spend my summers.

The first things to go from Minnicog were the water tanks in a strange looking flotilla one Thursday evening. The two giant water tanks one with the capacity of 8000 gallons, the other 5000 gallons that had been on Minnicog for forty-five years were being towed away to Penetanguishene. Their leaving was more simple than their arrival.

The machine age had come and Pete LePage, from Penetang, used a tow truck to move the tanks from their resting place on the crest of the island to a vantage point on the side hill. There he removed the holding cables, kicked free the blocks and the tanks rumbled and roared over the rocks toward the beach. They hit the water with a splash, sending a spume of spray twenty feet in the air.

I have been told it took nearly three weeks to bring the tanks from the water's edge to the top of the hill in 1910. The work then was all done by hand. They were manipulated on skids with block and tackle, heave, heave, slowly up the hill, over rough granite rocks and juniper bushes, past trees that grew tall over the passing years. After the tanks were in place there was the tremendous job of laying the miles of pipes, crisscrossing the rocks to the many buildings scattered around the hotel site.

Months, probably several years of labour altogether were undone in a matter of hours. On a Wednesday evening the dark green wooden buildings that housed the tanks was torn down. Thursday morning the truck arrived on a scow. The scow nudged up to the smooth shoreline on the far side of the main jetty. The gang plank was lowered and the truck was driven ashore.

The morning was beautiful. The sun, warm and the air was still. It was strange to hear the truck after several years without one on the island.

I was going about my usual morning chores when I heard the loud rumbling of a tank on the rough rocks. A runaway 8000 gallon tank crashed into the back of the Winter House.

I decided to go and see what was going on. I strolled up the rocks. By then the tow truck had a cable on the runaway and was holding it securely. But it appeared dangerous to me as it teetered on the edge of the rocks.

Slowly, the tank was worked down the steep incline, easing the tank and alternately blocking it with wood until it was within 30 feet of the shore. There all restraining lines were removed, letting the tank roll quickly until it hit the water with a loud smack. The men raced down after it and stood on the shore, watching the tank rolling back and forth until it settled quietly in the water. The tank was then towed to the side of the main jetty. The smaller tank was easier to handle and it made the trip to the water in less time.

A raft was made with lumber from the demolished tank house. The truck was loaded onto the scow, the tanks were jockeyed alongside the scow and lashed into position. They resembled huge pontoons towering above the height of the scow. Behind the scow was the raft of lumber held securely by the tow line of the truck.

It was a quiet evening when the tanks bade farewell to their island home. The sun was just slipping down behind the trees, painting the wispy clouds a fantasy of colours. Not a ripple troubled the face of Georgian Bay. The boat towing the flotilla roared and pulled forward. Its strange cargo followed at a surprising speed.

Bonnie and I walked to the high rock where we could watch the flotilla moving toward Penetanguishene. We watched as they made it through Gendron's Channel, heading out past Brébeuf light station.

The tanks were riding high. A little bit of Minnicog leaving us. The thing was done, the tank house and all it contained was gone.

I couldn't help thinking that the sun shouldn't be shining. The skies should have been pouring rain.

I remember the end. I remember these changes, changes that stirred outrage in my heart, changes I could do nothing to stop.

Next to come under the workmen's hands were the Nelles and Nimitz blocks - Upper and Lower Annexes in hotel days, barracks for hundreds of cadets over the years. Shingle after shingle, board after board, all the designated buildings came down.

A tractor hauled loads of lumber and material to the main jetty. People came from town to buy doors, windows and plumbing fixtures from the Cumming brothers. Frank did a lot of hauling for Ike and Bill to Peplars, Bates and to Honey Harbour.

As the work men closed in on the great Manor House I kept hoping that a miracle would save it. With its sweeping

verandahs and towering white chimneys the Manor House
had stood on the very summit of Minnicognashene for sixty-
three years.

It was a great house that had known years of glory and
grandeur and other years of neglect and disrepair.

The Manor House had stood against the gales off
Georgian Bay for over half a century. Years of rain had
washed its shingles. Winter snow had lain on its lofty roof.

This great house, standing at the top of this ancient
island, had become a landmark, a guide to the boatmen long
before the buoys marked the passageway of the Inside
Channel. It saw Indians in canoes make their way amongst
the islands selling their baskets and moccasins. Passenger
ships such as the *S.S. Waubic*, *Maud Davidson* and the
Midland City called daily at the docks with passengers and
supplies.

The guests that filled the great house were wealthy. Many
were famous. Minnicognashene was the most fashionable
summer resort on the shore.

I came to love the old house. I never tired of wandering
through its many rooms, pausing, here and there, to admire
the old-fashioned interior.

It was to the top story of this house that we would rush in
the spring to see how far the ice had broken in towards shore.
From the third floor we commanded a view of the
surrounding Bay as far as the eye could see. We watched for
the first lake freighters of the season coming out of Midland,
pushing their way through the heavy ice, moving out
through the gap until just their black smoke could be seen on
the far side of Giant's Tomb.

My hopes for the safety of the old house were crushed when the first shingles were torn from the roof. I turned away and could not bear to climb the hill to see it again.

I fled the island on the day the last chimney was pulled to the ground.

When I finally did climb the hill again, to stand beside the rubble and wreckage of a house that was built with pride so long ago, a building that had so well withstood the elements for so many years, I could not help but think that it wasn't just a house that had been torn down, but that a great era had ended and a part of the shore lay in ruins at my feet.

The End

Epilogue I

42

Once the Navy League shut down Minnicog, Frank went on to be a lighthouse keeper on the Great Lakes. When Frank retired, he spent his last years at the "House on the side-hill" in Sunnyside, Midland.

I wrote this when he left us.

Fare Thee Well

The head of our clan left us last week. He did not give us much warning and it has left us shattered. During the years I shared with this man of the shore and the Great Lakes I never knew him to hesitate about anything. Procrastination was my bad habit, not his.

He told me more than once that, when he was a little kid in Penetanguishene, he would rather ride the horses at the racetrack than go to school. That he went down the main street of the town, from the top of the hill, on roller skates because someone bet him he couldn't do it. His summers were spent with his family on Sara-Beck Island, near Somerset Island at Sans Souci where his father did carpentry work for a wealthy American.

When Grampa Rourke decided to abandon his tailoring business and move up the shore permanently, Frank gained the freedom he craved. He held on to it for the rest of his life.

Tinkering with a "one lunger" motor in a boat started him on the way to his great love for machinery. Frank could spend endless hours crouched over an engine, gas or diesel. Nothing could make him as grouchy as a motor that didn't work and there was no letting up until it was running perfectly.

Georgian Bay was his home before he was a teenager, the water his great love. He spent more time in a boat, rowboat, "one lunger" or magnificent yacht, than he did ashore. It was only natural that he become a Minor Waters Pilot and ply the channels and bays in supply boats, bringing a floating grocery store to the docks of the tourist population. He sailed the Lakes from the Lakehead to Erie long before his mariner sons were born, through Whitefish Bay when the ship was laden, not only with grain, but the decks with ice and snow. He worked on coal burning ships which swallowed tons of coal with only two coal passers to handle the job on six hour shifts. He was equally at home at either end of a ship, serving as helmsman on the *Midland City* or the pilot of Captain Ed Burke's *Westwind*.

Winter took him south of the border to work in Plymouth, Ohio, or into the lumber camps at Twelve Mile Bay. One winter was spent in the gold mining country of north-western Ontario, where they slept and ate under canvas at forty below zero. He went wolf hunting in the moonlight with his Indian friend Charlie Williams, played hockey on the windswept ice at Moose Point and carried mail on his back across the hills from MacTier. He played the fiddle and never missed a dance.

Frank told a friend he was going to marry me seven years before I was really aware he existed. He was right, of course. When I changed my name to Rourke it opened a door to adventure and excitement - to a way of life few others have known. A Gypsy life that made my mother shudder every time she thought about it.

We crawled on our stomachs over ice too thin to walk on; spent one of the happiest winters of our lives in a cabin close to Moon Falls; had a merry Christmas because Frank caught enough fur in his traps to buy gifts and the traditional bird.

I gave up skiing because he nearly split himself in half when he ran into a tree and I learned to spend the afternoon on the ice instead while he indulged in his favorite sport, ice-fishing. We would skate down river in the moonlight to visit my folks in Woods Bay.

We sailed a supply boat out of Midland the first year we were married. I learned to steer a thirty-five foot boat on a straight course whether I wanted to or not. I cried a bucket full of tears the first month. When Frank said steer straight for Red Rock or Pinery Point, he meant it. A zigzag course was beyond his comprehension. When Frank finally told me: "you are the most stubborn person I have ever trained but you are the best," I felt he had pinned a badge of honour on my sweater.

We took chances because we were young and sure. We came down the gap when the *Midland City* was tied up for heavy weather. I have slept with a life jacket for a pillow and canvas for a blanket when we had to give in to the elements. We travelled on pitch black nights when only Frank's knowledge of every twisting channel and hidden shoal made it possible.

He trained countless sailors to bring the navy ships from Minnicog to Midland when he was the pilot for National Defence at the Sea Cadet Camps. I often pitied the young

fellows but I knew they would be seamen when he was
finished.

We were in our element when we stood together on the
bridge of the *Alexander Henry* in the early spring. We seldom
looked back at the receding mainland as the *"Red Lady"* broke
her way through the ice. We looked outward at Cove Island,
anticipating the moment we would climb into the helicopter
on the flight deck for the flight over the choppy waters of
Lake Huron to the lightstation and nearly nine months of
isolation, freedom and a way of life we both loved.

Many places, many islands were our home during our
years on the Lakes, but we were never lonely. Loneliness
came only once to our lives and that was in December 1941
when Frank got his orders that he was going overseas with
the First Base Ordinance Workshop. Like many young men
at that time, he was a member of Canada's Armed Forces. It
took the huge contingent a long time to get over seas.

They were thirteen days at sea and chased back to Halifax
by U-boats. Two weeks rest in Truro Nova Scotia, then
silence until the 10th of March when word came: he was
somewhere in England. He was there for the blitz and
Dieppe. Scotland reminded him of Canada when he went to
visit my cousins. He came home, finally, on a hospital ship.
He was discharged a few months later and I can remember
laughing when he came through the door in an ill-fitting
civilian suit.

Frank seldom spoke about what went on overseas. He
closed doors quickly on the past and got on with the future.
He got busy on the Bay again. Before I knew it I was off to the
shore, to an island twelve miles from the mainland.

We had four sons and two daughters. He was proud of his children and trained them to take pride in themselves, their work and their families. He spoiled his two daughters a little, but encouraged his sons and daughters to be the best that they could be. His courage and determination are their heritage.

He left on his last great adventure early in the morning, perhaps to pilot a ship through the Milky Way or tend a lighthouse far out in the universe. Fare thee well Frank. We will think of you always. We will miss you always.

36 Frank Rourke

With love, good-bye

Epilogue II

43

The Rourke Clan to Date

Juanita Myers Rourke

Remained a widow for 18 years. She lived in the Midland area until moving west in 1982 to Mac Makenny's *Homeplace Ranch*, in Priddis Alberta, where she stayed for six years, helping to organize and run one of the best and most popular guest ranches in western Canada.

Juanita, having recovered from a grave illness, returned to Midland in 1988 and, with rare good fortune, became re-acquainted with an old and dear friend of both herself and Frank's, **Bev Keefe**, from Gendron's Channel. Bev, a well known local photographer, historian, teacher and former businessman and Juanita were married in the spring of 1992. Bev recalled, at their wedding, that the first time he saw Juanita she was putt-putting by in a little wooden boat with her children and he remembers thinking: "Now who is that pretty little woman with all those kids?"

Juanita and Bev are still pursuing the joys of Up The Shore at Gendron's Channel. Remarkably the cottage at Gendron's Channel includes the Rock Cottage which was bought and moved across the channel from Minnicog.

How little they suspected, when they moved the Rock Cottage off Minnicognashene how it would help bring Juanita full circle in her life up the shore.

The Family:

Glen Rourke
Married Anita Harrison of Midland
Two children, *Heather and Steven
*Expecting first grandchild
Hay River, North West Territories

Gail Rourke Lamoureux
Married Jack Lamoureux of Midland
Three children, Bill and *Chris Gostick and Jeff Lamoureux
Two grandchildren, *Kayla and *Kristen
Cambridge Bay, North West Territories and Midland, Ontario

Gary Rourke
Married Mardie Carruthers of Midland
Three children, Laura, Doug and Linda
Midland, Ontario

Bonnie Rourke
Married Murray Cayley of Toronto
Two children, *Paul and Todd Dumais
Three grandchildren, *Nicholas,*Tatiana,*Natasha
Calgary, Alberta

Garnet Rourke
Married Susan Richards of Midland
One child, Liam
Midland, Ontario

Gillard Rourke
Married Sandy Sheriff of Midland
Two children, Leigh and Sean
Midland, Ontario